GOD THE CREATOR OF THE UNIVERSE – HIS LEGAL MANUAL

M. PAUL DAS

GOD'S HEART-BEAT BE SEE IT, READ IT AND SENSE IT.

Book published by:

Kindle Direct Publishing (KDP)

This book is available at Amazon

GOD THE CREATOR OF THE UNIVERSE – HIS LEGAL MANUAL

Author Name: M. Paul Das

Kindle Direct Publishing (KDP)

ISBN-13 978-1-6939545-7-3

I STRONGLY FORWARD THIS BOOK TO ALL ON THE EARTH
TO SENSE HIM & HIM ONLY

WITHOUT ANY PRE-RESERVATION ANY ONE ENTER INTO THIS BOOK AND CONCEIVE HIM IN, CAN CERTAINLY ENTER IN HIM

IF YOU ARE WILLING TO SHARE
"YOUR EXPERIENCE WITH THIS BOOK",
PLEASE CONTACT
M.Paul Das (Author),
4th Floor, Sindhur Tower
160 / 95, Luz Church Road
Chennai-600 004, INDIA
E-mail to, mpauldas1@gmail.com
CELL: +91 9840 861 834,
+ 91 44-24993596

TO UNDERSTAND THE HEAVENLY JUDGE, SEE THE FLOW-CHART AND TO KNOW THE BIRTH OF THE BOOK SEE THE VIDEO IN - YouTube, F.B.
https://www.facebook.com/1454891728127707/videos/1544829499133929/

Video: facebook : "godcreatorbook"
YouTube: "GOD CREATOR BIRTH OF THE BOOK"

"GOD" - IS THE ONLY ONE
WHO searches the heart
and tests the mind,
and then compiles.

GOD- BY HIMSELF NULLIFIES, ALL THE JUSTIFIED CRIMES OF ANY ORDER, TO ANYONE, WHO IS `FOUND TO BE FIT,` IN HIS SIGHT, BECAUSE **HE** IS THE ONLY ONE HAVING, INFINITELY-INFINITE

SUPERNUMERARY

VISION & COMMISSION.

I thank `GOD` for **HIS** infinite love showered on me, to put forward **this book** `to the entire human race.` I beg to all on the earth, irrespective of Caste- Creed- Religion, Language,----------- etc- etc, to read this book, which will REVEAL HIS HEART BEAT, to understand **HIM**, what is **HIS** expectation, as a human. This eye opening will pull any one to walk on HIS TRACK. What at all required is, simply walk in `mercy and righteousness`, (Leaving all sort of learned emotions, principles, listening to various kind of variety of teachings of Religion, about Light, dark, etc, etc, blocking all the areas of illegal fond, fond on money etc, etc--) and step- up to walk upright, Instantly, such individual will,

DRAW, **HIS** PERSIONAL ATTENTION;

ULTIMATELY HE - will enter along the track, and then nothing is required

TO WIN THE WORLD.

(Author)

GOD-CREATOR - READ & REALISE

WHY THE SUN IS HOT?
WHY THE TREES AND GREENERIES OF
THE FOREST ARE BURNING?
WHY THE SEA WATER LEVEL RAISES?
WHY THE RAIN IS SHIFTING?
EVEN RAINING RESULTING DAMAGE
AND THEN STOPS.

**RECENT YEARS "MERCY AND RIGHTEOUS WALK"
IS DIMINISHING - RAPIDLY.**

KING OR RULERS OF ANY
COUNTRY
CANNOT HAVE TWO LAW BOOKS.
HOW, "THE CREATOR OF THE UNIVERSE"
can have, MULTI-LAW BOOKS ?
PLEASE CONCEIVE "THE INFINITE MERCY AND THE
GLORY OF RIGHTEOUS GOD",
*WHO ALONE HAS IMMORTALITY
DWELLING IN UNAPPROACHABLE LIGHT*

HE is the only ONE, WHO is looking for,
"those who are breathing in mercy and
righteousness, leaving all kinds of classifications
on the earth but running upright,
GOD IS THE ONE RUNNING BEHIND THEM.

LISTEN TO THE VOICE OF SUN, MOON AND THE
CALENDAR
A UNIQUE ALARM TO THE HUMAN RACE

5

 VOICE TO THE GLOBE

GOD - THE CREATOR AS SAVIOUR STRETCHES "HIS LEGAL MANUAL"

AS BOW STRING AND HIS MIGHT RELEASE THE *"ARROW"*

"GOD - THE CREATOR OF THE UNIVERSE - HIS LEGAL MANUAL".

THE **"ARROW OF HIS VOICE"** WILL PENETRATE THE EARTH SPHERE ALONG ALL DIMENSIONS; CROSSING THE BARRIERS OF CASTE, CREED, RELIGION, LANGUAGE ----.

IT ALSO TUNES THE STONY HEART OF THOSE WHO FIT TO STRETCH INTO FLESHLY HEART,

THEREAFTER ONLY, THE THINGS SAID IN HIS MANUAL WILL,
COME TO PASS.

AND HIS GREATEST WEAKNESS

A merciful one cries,
HE also cries.
Any righteous one falls,
HE also falls on him to protect
him and if he stands, HE is
nearer, to keep him to STAND.

**As long as the
righteous
stands
The Universe will
stand**

CREATOR IS MONITORING AND TRACKING THE INDIVIDUAL LIFE SPAN

THE INFINITELY-INFINITE  MY DAD, IS NOT A LOVER OF PRAISES, BUT HE COUNTS AND LOVES THE STEPS OF **"GOOD MEN".** EVEN THOUGH SUCH ONE FALLS, HE UPHOLDS HIM WITH HIS HAND. AGAIN HIS EYES ARE ON AND HIS EARS ARE OPEN TO THEIR CRY. IF MERCY AND RIGHTEOUSNESS ARE ASSOCIATED WITH ANY FAMILY-TREE, HE IS CONTINUOUSLY TRACKING AND MONITORING FOR THEIR TOILING LABOUR UNDER THE SUN.

So the energetic hours over which one is labouring may be
= 25 years, (Between, age, 25 to 50) x
5/7(Two days Holidays per week)
x 22/24 (Two hours travel)
x 16/24 (Eight hours sleep)
= (25x365.25 days) x (5/7) x (22/24) x (16/24) =3986, days = 95,664 (Hours), or say =1,00,000, hours

IF THE ABOVE LABOURING IS ASSOCIATED WITH MERCY AND RIGHTEOUSNESS, THEN IRRESPECTIVE OF CASTE, CREED, RELIGION, LANGUAGE-------, SUCH ONE WILL BE TREADING TOWARDS *HIS SPACE.E*

GREAT WARNING ALARM
TO ALL ON THE GLOBE

"ONE **NOAH** FOUND RIGHTEOUS IN THE SIGHT OF **GOD,** PREACHES ABOUT

THE RIGHTEOUSNESS OF GOD FOR
120 YEARS
UNTIL THEN FLOOD CAME AND
SWALLOWED THEM ALL,

AND ALL **LIVING BEINGS,** TREES AND PLANTS; ETC. ETC. **STILL THEN THEY NEVER SENSED.**

THE RESULTING PRODUCT IS
PETROL AND COAL.

IN THE SAME WAY------, "
"Matthew 24: 37-39"

OPEN HIS HEART AND SEE THROUGH

Do not rob the poor because he is poor,
Nor oppress the afflicted at the gate.
(Proverbs 22:22)

For the Lord will plead their cause,
And plunder the soul of those who plunder
them. (Proverbs 22:23)

One who increase his possessions by
usury and extortion, Gathers it for him who
will pity the poor. (Proverbs 28:8)

The righteous considers the cause of
the poor, But the wicked does not understand
such knowledge. (Prove. 29:7)

But the path of the just is like the
shining sun, That shines ever brighter unto
the perfect day. (Prove.rbs- 4:18)

He who oppresses the poor reproaches
his Maker , But he who honours Him has
mercy on the needy. **(**Prov:-14:31)

The righteous man walks in his
integrity, His children are blessed after him.
(Prove.rbs- 20:7)

Read Proverbs:
2:7, 3:12,32, 4:18, 10:29, 11: 12, 12:21, 12:28,
13:25, 15:9, 18:10, 19:22, 24:16, 28:27 ,29:7,27

ULTIMATE RESULT
OF
READING THIS BOOK

WHO EVER
ON THE EARTH READ THIS BOOK
WITHOUT ANY PRE-RESERVATION,
FOR SUCH ONE

THE CREATOR OF THE UNIVERSE,
WILL NOT BE HIDDEN ANY MORE.

BECAUSE OF HIS INFINITE MERCY, THE
GLORY OF HIM WILL VISIT THE
INDIVIDUAL TO WALK ON HIS TRACK.
FINALLY HE WILL BE LANDING

IN HIM AND IN HIM ONLY.

SUN	MOON

ASTRONOMICAL BODIES ALL AROUND

DIAMOND PLANET	MILKY WAY

SKY

"THE BOOK AND ITS TRACK"
IS ORIGINATED,
ORDERLY ALIGNED AND
PERFECTED
BY
ONE JUST ABOVE.

COMMENTARY BY "HIS" SCHOLAR
VICTOR GNANARAJ,
TRICHY
THIS IS A FANTASTIC BOOK---
A SMALL BOOK ,
BUT AN EXCELLENT BOOK;
MAKE TO TURN ABOUT TO RUN
TOWARDS THE RIGHT TRACK.

ACKNOWLEDGEMENTS

The Lord, GOD, found me fit to present this message, I Praise Him, and Praise Him. All Glory and Honour be to HIM and to HIM only.

LORD'S Servant, N. Sathu Paul Solomon called me by name on 29-08-2009, and revealed **GOD'S** plan in my life, for which I thank him from the depth of my heart. **LORD** preordained this message - Please read Chapter 16, Birth of the Book, View video in FACE BOOK- and YouTube.

I thank the **LORD'S** Servant, John Dhas from the depth of my heart, for he is the one whom **GOD** appointed, to pull me out to give this message.

Immediately after the message is spoken out from the platform, one Mr. Kamaraj commented that, **"this is the truth about GOD"**. So this will reach the world very slowly and this revelation by him is an unforgetful message given to me on that day. I thank Mr. Kamaraj and Mr. V. Silambarasan who motivated me to telecast the message.

I thank **Mr. Vikash Sharma of Rajasthan** for his desire to convey the message to his parents, and his enthusiasm made me to translate this message from **Tamil manuscript to ENGLISH BOOK** for which, I thank him personally. May **GOD** Bless Him.

GOD'S PLAN.

1). (i). **The whole book** is according to **Isaiah:** 61:11

(ii).**Very first para** of the book **Isaiah:** 40:5

(iii).**The last para** of the book, **Job, 28:26**

2). Prophecy by Eva. **PAUL** SOLOMON and again direct call by Pr. JOHN **DHAS.**

3). My name **"PAUL DAS"** is incorporated in their names.

M. Paul Das.   *(Read, 1 Corinthians 1:27)*

(GOD has chosen the *foolish* things of the world to put shame the **wise**, and *GOD* has chosen the weak things of the world to put to shame the things which are *mighty")*

(1 Corinthians 1:27)

CONTENTS
PLEASE READ CHAPTER- 17, LAST PARAGRAPH
FIRST

1. **CREATOR** AS **SAVIOUR**

2. TO WHOM THIS LEGAL MANUAL IS GIVEN.?
AND WHAT FOR GIVEN ?

3. WHO WILL UNDERSTAND HIS LEGAL MANUAL ?

4. GOD'S MERCY AND ITS DEPTH

5. FOUNDATION OF THE THRONE OF **GOD**

6. GLORY OF THE RIGHTEOUS **GOD**

7. KNOWLEDGE OF KNOWING **GOD**

8. WHY THE EYES OF THE RIGHTEOUS **LORD** RUN TO AND FRO THROUGHOUT THE WHOLE EARTH.?

9. WHAT WILL HAPPEN WHEN ONE WALKS IN **GOD'S** RIGHTEOUSNESS ?

10. THE RIGHTEOUS WORKS THAT PLEASE **GOD**

11. LORD'S WARNING TO HUMAN RACE

12. END TIME EVENTS

13. GLORY OF **GOD'S** CREATION

14. GLORY OF **GOD'S** RIGHTEOUSNESS

15. ESSENCE OF THE CREATOR'S LEGAL MANUAL

16. **LORD** PREORDAINED THIS MESSAGE TO TELL HIS GLORY TO THE HUMAN RACE

17. SACRIFICE OF **CREATOR** AS **SAVIOUR**

"REFER NEW KING JAMES VERSION" (NKJV)

PLEASE READ YOUR "LIFE", AT INTRODUCTION AND YOUR "LIFE TRAJECTORY" IN CHAPTER- 6

TO UNDERSTAND THE JUDICIARY OF THE EARTHLY JUDGE AND THE HEAVENLY JUDGE READ THE FLOW CHART AT THE END OF CHAPTER- 17

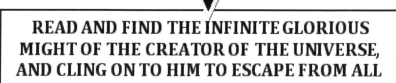

READ AND FIND THE INFINITE GLORIOUS MIGHT OF THE CREATOR OF THE UNIVERSE, AND CLING ON TO HIM TO ESCAPE FROM ALL PAIN AND VANITY.

A UNIQUE ALARM TO THE HUMAN RACE

THE CREATOR'S
LEGAL
MANUAL

Beloved ones,

Creator of the Universe is **online** to all the readers, viewers listening through **Book, Facebook, you tube**. We, the People of the world, when we **rejoice** on **HIS Mercy** and **Righteousness** , the **Word** which we meditate is charged by **HIS Glorious Spirit,** everyone will sense **HIS** Grace and Power from above. Thus the **word** of the Glorious Light penetrates through the ears of the **hearers and readers** and induce deep trust and passion in your hearts. Today you will experience that a **Glorious Light** is intercepting in your life.

In today's world, Mercy and Righteousness are slowly disintegrating and disappearing. The present mankind has not understood the Creator's Mercy and Righteousness, hence **"murder, theft, rape, divorce, ----------",** have become **rampant** in everyday life. Such incidents are reported in daily news papers and the news media. To escape from this evil, the only way is to understand   **"The Judiciary of the CREATOR-LORD-GOD."**

GOD, ONE WHO created all living beings, the sky, earth, ocean, sun, moon, stars and all galaxies and **HE** fixed an orbit for each one of them. **HE** is the one **WHO** shakes and quakes all of **HIS** creations according to **HIS** mercy and righteousness, because **"Righteousness and Justice are the Foundation of HIS throne"**, (Read. Chap.-5). In any country, **if righteousness and justice are in order, among the people of that land and the people in power;** then for such country the **sun light** and **the rain** are up to the pleasing level in the respective seasons, to meet the requirement of the land. (**Read chap-14**)

ONE WHO seeks a **human** of the **human** and this scene we can see in chap-8. Lastly look at the life track of a man till to the end and read the running track of the today's world in Chapter 12. As a Father from birth to end from generation to generation, **ONE Who** feeds, clothes, carries, watches, chastises, and punishes to fit as **HIS son,** according to **HIS** mercy and righteousness.

As I experienced The **Mighty CREATOR along my career,** so with only one message to the human race, which **HE** pre-planned and openly spoken out.

So, I stand in front of you to talk and write. The Book that I am holding, is **a Book** that does not belong to any sector but it is the **Creator's Legal Manual, WHO** created the **Universe** and it reveals **HIS HEART BEAT.**

Please read with patience. **I stand before you to declare that, this is the Creator's Legal Manual and I explain my stand as follows.**

IF A COUNTRY HAS TWO LAW BOOKS, THEN WHAT WILL HAPPEN ?

a). The **Judiciary** can't function, **Army** and **Police** force can't run their affairs and the system will collapse. This is accepted by all the people on this **planet earth**.

b). Similarly, if a King has two law books, then the **Judiciary** can't function, the **army** and **police** force can't run the State. The **Kingdom** will perish by itself.

When an unrighteous world can't have two Law Books, **GOD - ONE WHO** created the Universe, having Infinite Mercy and Righteousness, as the foundation of **HIS** throne, Who alone has immortality dwelling in an unapproachable Light, can have multi-LAW BOOKS ?

The people of the Universe have to read, **HIS Unique Law** and thus understand "HIS HEART BEAT"

Who created the Universe, and anyone likes to know **HIS majesty** in depth, please log on to **GOOGLE SEARCH**, type" **Milky Way Galaxy**", and see the **infinite wonders** of His creation, and realise **His infinite Majesty**.

NOW WE SEE THE UNIQUENESS OF "HIS LEGAL MANUAL."

WHEN WE LOOK AT IT EXTERNALLY:

(I) This Manual is not written by the spirit of man.

(ii) This is the only Manual, which is subjected to maximum number of **archaeological** investigations, which have historically proved its correctness and perfection.

(iii) This is the **first Manual**, which was printed by the **printing machine.**

(iv) This is the Manual which has been translated into maximum number of languages.

(v) Above all, this is the only Manual that reveals the **"Foundation of God's Throne".**

Now we will go through the Manual Internally:

1. First Chapter of the Manual explains the **creation,** and the last chapter reveals the end of the **world**, and the end of the **mankind.** (Revelation 20: 13)

2. This Manual demarcates the **LIGHT**, and the boundaries of **darkness.** (Isaiah 14: 12)

3. When the entire world was filled with **sexual sin, GOD'S** anchor was provoked and the whole creation was destroyed by **flood**. On that day the root of the **deep springs** were broken up and the windows of heaven were opened. (Genesis 7: 11)

4. When the cities were filled with **homosexuality**, the anger of **GOD rained brimstone and fire,** and those cities were totally consumed, which was terrible.
(Genesis 19: 24, 25)

5. The circumstances under which the Language was born. (Gen. 11:7)

6. Recent innovations like,

(i) Air has **weight,** (Job 28:25)

(ii) The earth is **spherical,** (Isaiah 40:22)

(iii)The earth **hangs** in the Universe, (Job 26:7)

7. Only Manual points out the location of human body to fix micro chips and the web "www." and its future, and several other facts were already recorded in this Manual, several thousand years ago.

GOD'S **Infinitely - Infinite, Might in Creation**
(i)   Human beings of All and All
(ii)   All living beings below the earth, from fungus to Crocodile.
(iii) Animals, ----Ant to Elephant.
(iv) Birds of all kinds.
(v) All beings inside the all living beings
(vi) Trees, Plants, etc. etc.
GOD is Feeding, Reading and Recording in Himself.

GOD'S – INFINITELY INFINITE WISDOM

The pinnacle of the wisdom of GOD is to fix gender to all living beings.

The First Chapter of **HIS** Manual progressively explains the **Creation**, and in this chapter we read,

"-----*A man shall leave his father and mother and be joined to his wife, and they shall become one flesh.*" (Genesis 2;24)

Moreover this Legal Manual established the boundaries, and disciplines between relationships, fixing whom one can or cannot have sex with, and such rulings are given as decree which becomes Commandments. So Creator's Legal Manual is also the Best Marriage Manual.

Any husband and wife, who are **bound** together in love, and live in accordance with **GOD'S** law of creation, can see that their **offspring** also attains the same decree or more of love and affection and more blessing in their family life.

This clause of the righteousness of **GOD**, is spread over the **earth sphere**, irrespective of caste, creed, religion, language----, and we can sense the same, when we deeply read the **history of families.**

LIFE

One who created man and woman, **Territory by Territory** and in the manner in which they are designed from **head to toe** is marvellous. Men are designed to be self productive for family, society, authorized to subdue and fill the earth in obedience to **CREATOR'S** pre-designated covenant, *"wed-lock"* for fruitful happy life and in turn to the offspring.

WED-LOCK: The (1) **consent** granted by the Creator thro' the (2) **law of the land** and society with the concurrence of (3) **parents** for the (4) **union of body and mind,** the most intimate relationship in its depth and intensity of (5) **two opposite sex** for (6) **oneness** and for (7) **healthy living**, through which the (8) **Sealed covenant** of **HIM** is released to raise the (9) **holy generation**.

Expansion: (Marked (1) to (9) in bracket), read below:

(1). **consent:** *Houses and riches are an inheritance from fathers, But a prudent wife is from the Lord.* (Proverbs- 19:14)

(2). **law of the land:** *By me kings reign And rulers decree justice.* (Proverbs-8:15)

(3). **parents:** *Honour your father and your mother, as the LORD your GOD has commanded you, that your days may be long, and that it may be well with you in the land which the LORD your GOD is giving you.*

(Deuteronomy- 5:16)

(4). **union of body and mind:** *For this reason a man shall leave his father and mother and be joined to his wife, and the two shall become one flesh.* (Ephesians-5:31)

5). **two opposite sex:** *You shall not lie with a male as with a woman. It is an abomination.*

(Leviticus, 18:22)

(6) **Oneness:** *The wife does not have authority over her own body, but the husband does. And likewise the husband does not have authority over his own body, but the wife does.* 1Corinthians. (7:4)

(7). **healthy living:** *Live joyfully with the wife whom you love all the days of your vain life which HE has given you under the sun, all your days of vanity; for that is your portion in life, and in the labour which you perform under the sun.* (Ecclesiastes-9:9)

(i) *Let your fountain be blessed, And rejoice with the wife of your youth.* (Proverbs-5:18)

(ii) *As a loving deer and a graceful doe, Let her breasts satisfy you at all times; And always be enraptured with her love.* (Proverbs-5:19)

(iii) *For they are life to those who find them, And health to all their flesh.* (Proverbs-4:22)

(8). Sealed covenant of Him: *Your eyes saw my substance, being yet unformed, And in Your book they all were written, The days fashioned for me, When as yet there were none of them.* (Psalm-139:16)

(9). holy generation: *But did HE not make them one, Having a remnant of the Spirit ? And why one? He seeks godly offspring, Therefore take heed to your spirit, And let none deal treacherously with the wife of his youth.* (Malachi-2:15)

KEY FOR VERY SUCCESSFUL LIFE:

Wives, submit to your own husbands, as to the LORD. (Ephesians-5:22)

Husbands, love your wives. --------- (Ephesians-5:25)

NOW WE GO THROUGH THE
"CREATOR'S LEGAL MANUAL"
CHAPTER BY CHAPTER
AS FOLLOWS

1. CREATOR AS SAVIOUR

When any author writes a book, first he writes an intro-duction. **In the preface** the author of the book will write about him and he summarizes the **purpose** of the book. **In the Conclusion one can see the essence of his writing.** Similarly in the first two chapters, the **CREATOR LORD GOD** explains **HIS** creation and the Purpose of **HIS** creation. The Book starts with (NKJV),

"In the beginning God created the heavens and the earth." (Genesis: 1:1)

Then **GOD** Said, "Let there be light: and there was light and **GOD** saw the light, that it was good: and **GOD** divided the light from the darkness", thus creation continues.

In order to understand the Lord and the essence of His writing, let's move on to the last chapter of His Manual, **Revelation.**

> *"I am the Alpha and the Omega, the Beginning and the End, the First and the Last."* (Revelation-22:13)

(Also read, **John-** 1:1, 14 **John-** 8: 24, Isaiah: 41:4, 43:10, 44:6, 48:12, **Revelation-** 1:8, 11)

The Existing **CREATOR** became the **SAVIOUR.**

To know more about Him let us see "**1-Timothy 3:16**",

> "*And without controversy great is the mystery of godliness: GOD was manifested in the flesh-----*"　　　　　　　　　(*1-Timothy 3:16*)

> "*He was clothed with a robe dipped in blood, and HIS name is called "The Word of GOD".*
> (Revelation- 19:13)

This is how this Legal Manual was **sanctified** through the **HOLY BLOOD**.

To realise that **HE** is the "**CREATOR AS SAVIOUR**", let me share some standing evidences, with all the readers, viewers of this programme.

The CREATOR revealed as SAVIOUR
<u>to the Universe in a unique manner.</u>

1. Not only the Creator's Legal Manual, but also the **Quran, Chapter 19,** Mariam, Surah 21 says, - By **GOD'S** Command, **HE** was conceived in a **Virgin**.

2. Let me explain the **MAJESTY and UNIQUENESS** of **HIS** birth. If we consider

(i) The average age of a person is 60 Years,

(ii) In one generation about *30 crore at starting of the Era. and 780 crore* people are at present on the earth,

(iii) From the beginning of the era up to 2020 years about 34 Generations and so,

(iv) The total population up to 2020 years may be =34x(30+780)/2= **13,770**, **Crore (AC)**, people have born. Remember that all these people are born as a result of the unity of the parents or in other words they all belong to **one genealogy**.

But *"Who being the Brightness of His Glory and the Express Image of His Person ---*
--------------------------------- " (Hebrews 1:3)
Conceived in a **Virgin** in another genealogy with unique blood group and the name of **HIS** blood group is *"Holy"*. By **HIS** **unique holy Virgin birth, HE** distinguishes **HIMSELF** from all other men. So readers and viewers, I urge you to think, whether is it right, to compare **HIM** with any other human being in the Universe.

---

3. When HE was born, history blast off Into two. (BC, AD)

4. Further **LOOK THE CALENDER DATE, in front of you,** which conveys a message that **SAVIOUR** was born, **SO MANY years, months and days ago from Today.** This truth is being conveyed by the Calendar to all people on this Earth every day. Whether they sense it or not, the Calendar is constantly speaking. **It is a constant witness.**

5. Further, we see that the date founded on HIS birth is the base used to tune all inventions beyond *ALL CATEGORY OF COMPUTERS, SATELLITES, ROCKETS,----- ETC. ETC.* Great men of this world or Great Rulers of this world, do not have this Glory: Why? Please keep thinking.

6. Also when any one with deep trust and faith in heart, from any part of the world is using **HIS** Holy Name, demons cry and fly away knowing that **HE** is "**THE CRE-ATOR AS SAVIOUR,**" pronouncing that **HE is the LORD**. In the same way, from those who have deep understanding and trust in heart, then disease will disappear, new organs of the body are created, the blind see, the deaf hear, the lame walk. Just think why this happens when **HIS** name is pronounced!

2. TO WHOM THIS LEGAL MANUAL IS GIVEN? AND WHAT FOR GIVEN?

"--- He has made from one blood every nation of men to dwell on all the face of the earth, and has determined their pre-appointed times and the boundaries of their dwellings. Acts -17:26, (NKJV)

So that they should seek the Lord, in the hope that they might GROPE for HIM and find HIM, though HE is not far from each one of us." Acts -17:27 (NKJV)

(*LEGAL MANUAL*) WHAT FOR GIVEN ?

HE who walks righteously and speaks uprightly, He who despises the gain of oppressions, Who gestures with his hands, refusing bribes,Who stops his ears from hearing of bloodshed, And shuts his eyes from seeing evil : (*Isaiah-33:15)*

He will dwell on high: HIS place of defence will be the fortress of rocks : Bread will be given him, His water will be sure. (*Isaiah-33:16)*

Likewise **GOD** created all people on the earth by **one blood** irrespective of caste, creed, religion, language --- and **HE** determined their pre-appointed times and the boundaries for their dwellings. **HE** is not far away from each one of us, but **HE is closer to those who walk in GOD'S MERCY and RIGHTEOUSNESS. As darkness covers the earth, HIS Legal Manual shows the way to Grope for HIM and to find HIM.**

3. WHO WILL UNDERSTAND HIS LEGAL MANUAL

When an **atheist** reads this book, from the first page to the last page, because the book explains the **might** of **GOD** and His miraculous works, as " **he cannot understand that the Lord's might divided the Red sea**", he would want to turn this **book** into ashes. That's what **Hitler**, the man behind the Second World War did. The same thing was done by **Walter.** Walter said that within his lifetime he will destroy this book and that it will not be known to the people any more. But do you know what happened after his death, his house itself was turned into a **printing press,** where the "**CREATOR'S LEGAL MANUAL**" was printed.

But when a righteous one reads this book, who is a righteous man, "a person who practices **mercy, righteousness** with a desire to please **GOD**, and lives according to **GOD'S will**", irrespective of caste, creed, language, religion----------, and if such a person intercepts **HIS BOOK,** he will carry it in his **arms**, in his **heart** and in his **mind.**

The total **crores** of population living on the earth, read **HIS LAW-BOOK,** Each one will Know **HIM** and understand **HIM,** in his own way the individual is **found to be fit.** The related words we can see in the continuing page.

This is the "**KEY**" for opening
"**THE CREATOR'S LEGAL MANUAL**"

"HE stores up sound wisdom for the upright;
He is a shield to those who walk uprightly."
(Proverbs -2:7)

"--------But HIS secret council is with the
upright"   (Proverbs -3:32)

"Knowing this: that law is not made for a
righteous person, ----------"   (1Timothy -1:9)

Read ISAIAH, 28:13 and understand, why?, the Law-Book is blind to the eyes of unrighteous person and its depth, and thus understand HIS HEART.

The LORD GOD has kept the sound wisdom for the righteous man. What is sound wisdom? It is Knowing GOD'S might, understanding the personality of GOD, what HE can do and what HE can't, what HE likes and what HE hates. But this sound wisdom is not given to all. But it is given to those who understand GOD'S righteousness and mercy, and it is given in proportion to their understanding.

ISAIAH,28:13, makes it clear to understand

That is, if one
having spectacle,
fitted with two lenses of
mercy and righteousness

and for such one looks through **those lenses**, for him **HIS Legal Manual** will **look, brighter and brighter,** and so he will understand its depth, and conceive **HIM** in **BETTER AND DEEPER .**

GOD'S RIGHTEOUSNESS IS KNOWN TO ALL BEINGS THAT HAS BREATH.

"Let everything that has breath, praise the Lord. Praise the Lord." (Psalms- 150: 6)

"But now ask the beasts, and they will teach you; And the Birds of the air, and they will tell you;

(Job- 12:7)

Or speak to the earth, and it will teach you; And the fish of the sea will explain to you. (Job- 12:8)

His thunder declares it, The cattle also, concerning the rising storm. (Job- 36:33)

Let us observe together, all living beings in this world. The **wild animals, the birds, the reptiles, the amphibians**- all of them when they see the **dawn** of a new day, they lift up their eyes and are eagerly looking to see the **CREATOR.**

(I) The **lion** comes out of its den, lifting up its eyes above and roars.

(ii) The **birds** chirp, in praise of **HIS** name, crows move together and rejoice.

(iii) **The rabbit is** coming out of its burrow, and is lifting up its eyes.

(iv) **Fish** jumps out of the water, looking unto the sky and goes back into the water.

Why do they do so? It is because they know one thing, ie. they know their **CREATOR** , even though they lack the sixth sense. When HE commands the living creatures of mountainous forests, marshy lands, shore, etc. etc....., they are entering into the human territory to execute **HIS** order, from the beginning too -------.

WHAT GOD RESERVED FOR ITS UNDERSTANDING?

(i). In their life time, **they never work for their food, it is already provided for, simply to run off or fly to eat.**

"The eyes of all look expectantly to you, And You give them their food in due season. (Psalm-145:15)

You open Your hand and satisfy the desire of every living thing." (Psalm-145:16)

What do these living beings again gain, because of their knowledge of **GOD**?

(ii). In their lifetime they do not go to a doctor, and

(iii). In their life time they never seek a doctor for delivery.

But humans who have a sixth sense, when fall sick, they are seeking the doctor first, and the **CREATOR** gets the second position in their priority. Though we don't seek **GOD, HE** still finds us and treats us through the doctors. Let's consider a critical asthmatic patient. The steroid injection, which controls breathlessness of one **asthmatic** patient, becomes a killer for another patient. Similarly a drug given for a particular disease, which heals one and for the same disease, **the same drug is allergic to another.**

We can understand **one basic thing** from this that without **GOD'S** will, medicine or treatment cannot heal a patient. I have realised this truth, each and every day of my life, amidst of all my varying ailments.

Any **specialist,** from any honourable Institution in the world, cannot know the **total number** of **living cells** in anyone's body. All the living cells are waiting for **GOD.**

They act together as per HIS command. That is why a person, who goes to bed very healthy, rises up in the morning with **various ailments.**

Whereas a person for whose days are numbered, conformed by the Doctors is living more years after that, in spite of the missing organs, and their faulty functions. Several such medical miracles happen every day, for which no medical or scientific explanation is available.

GOD'S RIGHTEOUSNESS IS YET TO REACH THE MANKIND
How **GOD'S** infinitely-infinite wisdom controls the people on the earth **from the beginning.**

In whose hand is the life of every living thing, And the breath of all mankind. (Job- 12:10)

Wisdom is with aged man ,And with length of days, understanding . (Job- 12:12)

He loosens the bonds of kings, And binds their waist with a belt. (Job- 12:18)

He leads princes away plundered, And overthrows the mighty. (Job- 12:19)

He takes away the understanding of the chiefs of the people on the earth, And makes them wander in a pathless wilderness. (Job- 12:24)

4. GOD'S MERCY AND ITS DEPTH

"Yet HE is not partial to princes, Nor does HE regard the rich more than the poor; -----"

(NKJV - Job - 34:19)

Just visualize the wealth of our **CREATOR- LORD-GOD**, Who has so much regard for the **poor**. HE is the GOD Who crystallized the formation of diamond & jasper in rock. HE is the **LORD, WHO** has dissolved the ores of gold, silver and valuable minerals in earth and **precious grains** in sand. **HE** is the **Owner** of **50, 000, Crore** Galaxies Including **Diamond Planet** containing only diamond.

Please conceive the **Melting Heart of One Who embraces all on the street**. Know **HIM** and understand **HIM**, how "**HIS MANUAL**" explains the **HEART OF THIS AMAZING CREATOR**. Let the humans look at **HIM**, look at **HIM**.

Let us look at a poor man, who spends his night aside of the street. **He does not have any religion.** He goes to sleep thanking the **LORD** for that day and asking **HIS** help for the next day's food. On the contrary, let us look at any one of the richest persons in the world. He is praying to **GOD** that, he has to get **10, 000-crores** in a few days, and if he gets that amount, he will **give** back to **GOD, 1000 crores.** This is what the whole people of the world and **all the Religions** in the world are doing. They are thinking that if they give to **GOD, GOD** will pay back in manifold. When **GOD** comes down from **HIS** Glory to meet these two people, **HE** will **meet the poor one first** according to **Luke-16:19 to 23**. But **HE** may not meet the rich one as he put condition to **GOD.**

On the contrary, if these two are going to meet the **President of a Nation,** the rich person is honoured and taken to see the President. But at the same time, police will not permit the **poor** man to enter the neighbourhood. **GOD** has already said this in **Isaiah-55:9.**

"For as the heavens are higher than the earth, So are My ways higher than your ways, And My thoughts than your thoughts."

THE DEPTH OF HIS HEART
He who oppresses the poor reproaches his Maker, But he who honours HIM has mercy on the needy. (Proverbs- 14:31)

Whoever shuts his ears to the cry of the poor, Will also cry himself and not be heard. (proverbs- 21:13)

Further- *Psalm:* **41:1-3,** *68:10, Prov: 19:22,* **22:22-23,** *28:27, 29:7*

HE IS GENUINE BECAUSE HE IS TRACKING

"For HE has not despised nor abhorred the affliction of the afflicted; Nor has HE hidden HIs face from HIM; But when he cried TO HIM, HE heard." (Psalam-22:24)

Let me explain this. A person becomes sick, because of wounds in his **intestine,** a foul odour emits from his body. His wife serves him food. But because of the emission of bad odour, she **looks down** upon him, and if his condition becomes worse and his appearance distorted, his wife develops **hatred** towards him. As days go by and his situation becomes worse, she just pushes the food into his room, and ask him to take and eat. That is, she change herself from feeding to ordering and thus she **hides** her face. In these circumstances, if the **sick one** cries out to **GOD** realising his sinful life, **LORD-GOD ALMIGHTY** moves with compassion, and comes down from **HIS Throne** to visit him.

HE never looks down upon him. **HE** never hates and **HE** does not hide **HIS** face. **HE** will immediately either heal him or take him to **HIS** Glory. Either is easy for the **LORD** and thus **HE** brings his misery to an end.

MERCY TRIUMPHS OVER JUDGEMENT

"For Judgement is without mercy to the one who has shown no mercy. Mercy triumphs over judgement." (James-2.13)

I will explain this with a real incident. A thief walks on the street with an intention to steal. He saw a big house and steals jewelleries from that house and he disappears. Actually the house which he has **stolen** was a Judge's house. Since it was the Judge's house, the police force was activated and the thief was arrested in a week's time, and he was brought to the Court. As soon as the Judge saw him, the Judge started thinking of giving a severe punishment to the thief for his crime. During the enquiry, the thief said, "I am a very poor man, my neighbour was going through a great agony; yes, I have stolen the things but I never knew that it was the Judge's house; I did not use them but I gave them to the neighbour". This made the Judge to rethink, "can I consider him as a robber", as he has not retained the things with him.

The Judge may give a little punishment, or release him as he has not done this for himself but for the neighbour. Much more is the compassion of our **CREATOR**. If we show mercy, we will also receive **Mercy on that Day**.

He who has pity on the poor lends to the LORD, And HE will pay back what he has given.

(Proverbs-19:17)

He who gives to the poor will not lack, But he who hides his eyes will have many curses.

(Proverbs-28:27)

IF ANY ONE'S HEART IS WET, SUCH ONE WILL BE FIT TO DRAW NEARER TO HIM, IF NOT WILL BE LEFT-OUT.

---

5. FOUNDATION OF THE THRONE OF GOD

" *Righteousness and justice are the foundation of YOUR throne; "* (Psalm- 89:14, **NKJV**)

<u>WHAT IS SUSTAINING HIM?</u>

"-----And HIS own righteousness, it sustained HIM." (Isaiah- 59:16)

<u>PERFECTION OF HIS JUDGEMENT!</u>

"Also I will make justice the measuring line, And righteousness the plummet--------". (Isaiah- 28:17)

"To do righteousness and justice
Is more acceptable to Lord than sacrifice" (Proverbs:- 21-3)

Also read;Judges-1:6,7-read it and conceive it"

<u>WHY HE IS THE MOST HIGH?</u>

"But the LORD of hosts shall be exalted in judgment, And GOD who is holy shall be hallowed in righteousness." (Isaiah-5:16)

In righteousness, see the glory of the Holy **GOD**. **HE is the ONE, WHO is dwelling in "unapproachable light"**-and because of **HIS** impartial righteousness, the **LIGHT OF GLORY AROUND HIM SHINES BRIGHTER AND BRIGHTER.**

WHERE IS HIS RIGHTEOUSNESS?"

------ --- -YOUR right hand is full of right-
eousness   *(Psalm-48:10)*

HOW MUCH HIS HEART IS MELTING AS A FATHER!

"A father of the fatherless, a defender of the widows, Is GOD in his holy habitation."

(Psalm- 68:5)

Wherever **injustice** happens to the **orphan**, or to a **widow**, or any poor one, don't think they are destitutes. **THE MIGHTY ONE- THE FOUNDER OF THE UNIVERSE, WHO stands with them as father, comes down from HIS, MIGHTY THRONE** to deliver the judgement against the culprit, blocking his ways at the appropriate place, in **HIS** predestined time.

WHAT GOD EXPECTS FROM A MAN?

"He has shown you, O man, what is good; And what does the Lord require of you ,But to do justly, To love mercy, And to walk humbly with your God."

(Micah-6:8)

*Listen to what the **LORD- GOD** is seeking. **HE** is calling us to do justice, sho*w mercy to the needy, walk before the **LORD** in humility and be righteous in all of our ways. To walk on this track, **the man is planted on this earth planet.**

Ne- Bu- Chad- Nez'zar:

How the Emperor of the Great Babylonian Kingdom has experienced **GOD?** He was the king who built the **Hanging Garden of Babylon, one of the wonders of the world.** When he was walking in the **Royal Palace of Babylon,**

The king spoke, saying, "Is not this great Babylon, that I have built for a royal dwelling by my mighty power and for the Honour of my majesty?"

(Daniel-4:30)

While the word was still in the king's mouth, a voice fell from heaven:" King Ne-bu-chad- nez'zar, to you it is spoken: the kingdom has departed from you !"
(Daniel-4:31)

Accordingly he lost his kingdom he was wandering like a cattle in the wilderness and **ate grass.** Then he realized the error in his arrogance and pride, then he lifted his eyes to **Heaven** and then he got **exalted back** to the throne, now he **raised his voice as,**

"Now I, Ne-bu-chad-nez'zar, praise and extol and honour the king of heaven, all of whose works are truth, and His ways justice. And those who walk in pride HE is able to put down.

(Daniel-4:37)

All are under **HIS vision, and commission,** even a **king** can't escape.

HUMAN RACE IS NOT IN A POSITION TO ACKNOWLEDGE GOD'S RIGHTEOUSNES

Why mankind is unable to understand **LORD GOD'S** mercy and righteousness ? The reason is that **HE** is full of mercy over and above 99%, but **HE** pronounces judgement on less than 1%,   **(Exodus 34:6, 7)** and so man's mind dares to do evil. This we can see in,

"Because sentence against evil work is not executed speedily, therefore the heart of the sons of men is fully set in them to do evil."

(Ecclesiastes-8:11)

" Do not be deceived. GOD is not mocked: for whatever a man sows, that he will also reap.   *(Galations 6:7)*

It is a joy for the just to do justice. But destruction will come to the workers of iniquity *(Proverbs-21:15)*

The righteous considers the cause of the poor, But the wicked does not understand such knowledge. *(Proverbs : 29:7)*

READ MORE FOR HIS MERCY AND RIGHTEOUSNESS, TURN TO,

Proverbs- 29:7, 27, Micah-6:8, Hosea-12:6, **Luke -7:29**, **Matthew-21:31, 32**, Matthew-23:23, Luke-11:42, Romans-6:18, 20, **Romans-10:3, 10:20**, **Isaiah-65:1, 1 Jon-2:29, 3:7**, 2Peter-2:5, Hebrews-5:13, **Hebrews-6:1to8.**

6. GLORY OF THE RIGHTEOUS
GOD

THE CREATOR OF ALL CREATION-WHERE HE IS DWELLING?

"Who alone has Immortality dwelling in unapproachable light----".
(1Timothy- 6:16)

HE is the **ONLY ONE** dwelling in un-approachable light, having **INFINITELY-INFINITE, WISDOM,** commanding about 50,000, Crore Galaxies, each one is elliptically encircled by Billion--Billion, Stars. At any moment each and every point of ALL Galaxies as a whole is on **HIS VISION** and **COMMISSION**, with- out laps of **a fraction of a second.**

Other Hand. HE is the only one having HIS   ruling over the Entire Galaxical Mass as a whole, Stars, all Astronomic bodies, all living creatures, both men and cattle and all beasts, creeping things, birds of all kinds etc, etc., HE is the Only One seeing, observing and recording in HIM SELF from the beginning to--------------------------.

Behold happy is the man whom GOD corrects:
Therefore do not despise the Chastening of the
ALMIGHTY.   *(Job-5:17)*

For HE bruises , but HE binds up; He wounds,
but HIS hands make whole.   *(Job-5:18)*

HE removes the mountains, and they do not know ,when
HE overturns them in HIS anger: *(Job-9:5)*

HE shakes the earth out of its place
And its pillars tremble.   *(Job-9:6)*

HE commands the sun, and it does not rise:
HE seals off the Stars;   *(Job-9:7)*

HE alone spread out the heavens ,
And treads on the waves of the sea;   *(Job-9:8)*

HE made the Bear , O'ri'on and the
Plei' a-des, And the chambers of the south :   *(Job-9:9)*

HE does great things past finding out,
Yes, wonders without number.   *(Job-9:10)*
====================================
=============================*Etc, Etc.*

The earth is given in the hands of the wicked.
HE covers the faces of its judges,
If it is not HE, who else could it be?   **(Job-9:24)**

     In day to day life, **GOD** is the one Who lifts us from the soaking pit, and to understand the **MIGHT of HIS HAND**, whereas the **opponent** is the hand of darkness, who pushes us into the pit, and here we will see the same through physical **light** and **darkness** around us. The role of light and darkness is explained thro'out - **HIS MANUAL.**

LIGHT-(L)	DARK
1. The **Light** is surmounted By **"Glory"**, ie., the light is encircled by **"Glory"**.	The darkness is surrounded by **"Gory"**. (In the word **Glory**, If light,"**l**" is absent, then it becomes **"Gory"**). Referring the dictionary, for the meaning of **"Gory"**, it reads as **blood-thirsty, drenched in blood----**.
2. In **Light** we know where we are and the path in front of us.	In darkness we are not aware of the location and the way ahead.
3. **Light** , destroys darkness.	Darkness can't destroy **Light**.
4. In **Light,** If our dress has a stain, it is exposed.	In darkness the stain will be covered by darkness.

5. a) Let us take an empty vessel, and fill it with water, then the shape of water is nothing but the shape of the vessel.

b) If we empty the vessel and close it with a lid, then darkness is inside and it becomes the shape of the vessel.

c) If we put a hole on the vessel, light beam enters, ie. if we give way then only light enters, otherwise vessel shape as darkness inside. ie. Without mercy and righteous walk LIGHT never enter in.

Further the **LORD** allowed us to swing according to our freewill in an open orbit between the ***birth - death terminals*** applicable to all people on the earth and is plotted as a *graph.*

LIFE TRACK..

Please *read the graph in the next page* and the parameter of the *graph is given below.*

(i). Origin, at (0,0). **(It is the birth Terminal)**

(ii).   Apex point **1**(x, y), is any one's peak period in his life time, for the parameters given vertically along **Y**-axis.

(iii).The curve meeting point on, **X**-axis, Is the end of fleshly life of all . **(End terminal)**

The curve connecting all the three   points, is *nothing but **a second degree parabola.***

GRAPH IS THE TRACK OF EVERY HUMAN.
**Please read the graph and
RIGHTLY UNDERSTAND**
THE ONE WHO TRACKS US, BE EVER REMEMBERED
**TO LAND ON
HIS TRACK.**

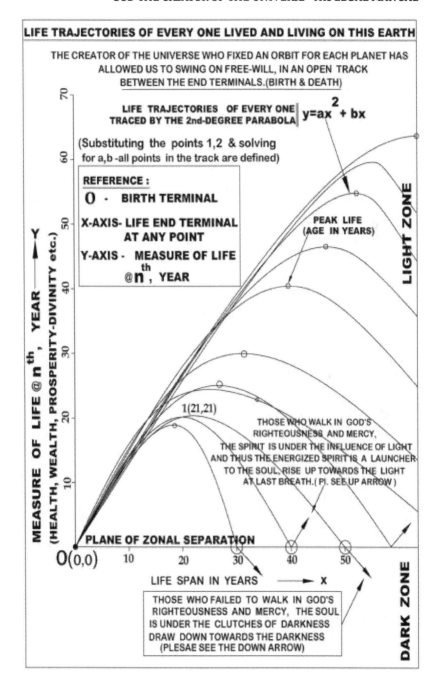

LIFE TRAJECTORIES OF EVERY ONE LIVED AND LIVING ON THIS EARTH

THE CREATOR OF THE UNIVERSE WHO FIXED AN ORBIT FOR EACH PLANET HAS ALLOWED US TO SWING ON FREE-WILL, IN AN OPEN TRACK BETWEEN THE END TERMINALS.(BIRTH & DEATH)

LIFE TRAJECTORIES OF EVERY ONE TRACED BY THE 2nd-DEGREE PARABOLA $y=ax^2 + bx$

(Substituting the points 1,2 & solving for a,b -all points in the track are defined)

REFERENCE :

O - BIRTH TERMINAL

X-AXIS- LIFE END TERMINAL AT ANY POINT

Y-AXIS - MEASURE OF LIFE @n^{th}, YEAR

PEAK LIFE (AGE IN YEARS)

LIGHT ZONE

MEASURE OF LIFE @ n^{th}, YEAR (HEALTH, WEALTH, PROSPERITY-DIVINITY etc.)

1(21,21)

THOSE WHO WALK IN GOD'S RIGHTEOUSNESS AND MERCY, THE SPIRIT IS UNDER THE INFLUENCE OF LIGHT AND THUS THE ENERGIZED SPIRIT IS A LAUNCHER TO THE SOUL, RISE UP TOWARDS THE LIGHT AT LAST BREATH.(PI. SEE UP ARROW)

PLANE OF ZONAL SEPARATION

$O(0,0)$

LIFE SPAN IN YEARS ⟶ X

THOSE WHO FAILED TO WALK IN GOD'S RIGHTEOUSNESS AND MERCY, THE SOUL IS UNDER THE CLUTCHES OF DARKNESS DRAW DOWN TOWARDS THE DARKNESS (PLESAE SEE THE DOWN ARROW)

DARK ZONE

49

7. KNOWLEDGE OF KNOWING GOD

Now the human life, becomes a race, running as fouler, deviating from their own track, and also become hunters. In their walk and talk they defile themselves and so they become the mockers of the MAKER. The knowledge about the CREATOR alone can make one to stand peaceful.

Thus says the Lord: "Let not the wise man glory in his wisdom, Let not the mighty man glory in his might, Nor let the rich man glory in his riches: (Jeremiah-9:23)

But let him who glories glory in this, That he understands and knows Me, That I am the LORD, exercising loving kindness, judgment, and righteousness in the earth. For in these I delight" says the LORD. (Jeremiah-9:24)

In the whole of GOD'S Manual, GOD permits man to be proud of knowing that GOD is the ONE exercising loving kindness, righteousness and justice on this planet earth.   The unrighteous king who ruled the kingdom, to whom the LORD GOD said:

"Shall you reign because you enclose yourself in cedar? Did not your father eat and drink, And do justice and righteousness? Then it was well with Him.

(Jeremiah-22:15)

He judged the cause of the poor and needy; Then it was well. Was not this knowing Me?

Says the LORD." (Jeremiah-22:16)

I, the Lord, search the heart, I test the mind, Even to give every man according to his ways, According to the fruit of his doings. (Jeremiah-17:10)

GOD IS THE ONE, LOVING THE RIGHT HUMANS ON THIS EARTH <u>AS HIS SONS & DAUGHTERS</u>

If you endure chastening, GOD deals with you as sons : for what son is there whom a father dos not chasten? (Hebrews-12:7)

But if you are without chastening, of which all have become partakers, then you are illegitimate and not sons. (Hebrews-12:8)

The righteous perishes, And no man takes it to heart; Merciful men are taken away, While no one considers, That the righteous is taken away from evil. (Isaiah.57:1)

He Shall enter into peace: They shall rest in their beds, Each one walking in his uprightness. (Isaiah. 57:2)

GOD IS THE ONE, LOVING
<u>*THE RIGHTEOUS NATION*</u>

I was sought by those who did not ask Me; I was found by those who did not seek Me. I said, Here I am, To a nation that was not called by My name. (Isaiah.65:1)

FURTHER READ:-

Jeremiah.10:12, Mathew. 15:9, Isaiah.29:13,
Psalm.125:3, Jeremiah. 4:22, 5:30, 31, 6:13,
7:4. 1Chronicles.28:9, Jeremiah.17:10,

Romans. 2:11 to 16, 1Timothy.1:9,

Hebrews.4:13, 6:1-8, 12:7, 8: Job: 36:7

WHY THE MAN FAILS TO REMEMBER THAT "THE LIFE IS SHORT?"

*"------, because GOD   keeps him busy with
the joy of his heart".*   (Ecclesiastes. 5:20)

(Also read Ecclesi, 2:24, 5:19)

---

8. WHY THE EYES OF THE RIGHTEOUS LORD RUN TO AND FRO THROUGHOUT THE WHOLE EARTH

The human is travelling from one end of the globe to the other end, from the plain to the top of mountainous hillock to seek "**GOD- THE CREATOR**". But **HIS EYES** run to and fro throughout the whole earth to seek a **Human** of the human, and this scene we can see now.

"For the eyes of the Lord run to and fro throughout the whole earth, to show Himself strong on behalf of those whose heart is loyal to Him.   (2Chronicles 16:9)

If one who realises and knows that the **Lord** is righteous, and **HE** is infinite in truth,------ and **HE** is infinitely good------, then the **LORD** comes down from **HIS** Glories Throne in search of such people, irrespective of any religion, caste, creed, language------. This we can see throughout **HIS** Manual.

WHO WILL DWELL WITH HIM?

"My eyes shall be on the faithful of the land, That they may dwell with me; -- --------".   (Psalm- 101:6)

GOD is in search of faithful persons in every country, every state, every city, every town and in every village. When **HE** finds such a person, what **HIS** Manual says "**MY EYES shall be on him**". That is the **LORD GOD** follows him, leads him towards a fruitful life, and bring him up, and reveals the knowledge about **HIM**, and finally take him to keep under **HIS GLORY.**

53

WHO IS ACCEPTABLE TO HIM?

"About the ninth hour of the day he saw clearly in a vision an angel of God coming in and saying to him, "Cornelius".
(Acts -10: 3 to 5)

And when he observed him, he was afraid, and said, "What is it, Lord?", So he said to him, "Your prayers and your alms have come up for a memorial before GOD.
(Acts- 10: 4)

Now send men to Jop'pa, and send for Simon, whose surname is Peter: "
(Acts- 10: 5)

GOD of mercy comes down from **HIS** throne, sent an **angel** as messenger and **he** gives the address of **St. Peter**, and this St. Peter when reached "Cornelius" house, he speaks out, **Acts- 10:34 & 35.**

"Then Peter opened his mouth and said: "In truth I perceive that GOD shows no partiality."
(Acts- 10:34)

" But in every nation whoever fears HIM and works righteousness is accepted by HIM."
(Acts- 10:35)

Please listen to the words spoken by St. Peter, **LORD ALMIGHTY** does not have any partiality over the people on the land, but one who fears and walks in righteousness is accepted by **HIM**.

PANDIT DHARM PRAKASH SHARMA

In our Mother Land of **Bharath**, during our days, **GOD-THE CREATOR'S** eyes followed one man and the **LORD** intercepted in his Life.

His name is **Pandit Dharm Prakash Sharma from Rajasthan.** I had the privilege of listening to his **autobiography**, spoken out by him, on 11 April 2010 at Chennai.

He was the head of the Rajasthan Congress Party, during the Period of **Indira Gandhi's** Prime Ministership. He resigned from that position after his encounter with The **LORD GOD.** His father was the **Chief Acharya** for **Pushkar Peedam,** comprising of **420 temples. His parents spent six years in jail along with Mahatma Gandhiji, for supporting the freedom fight movement. So he spent 6 years of his childhood, in Gandhiji's Ashram.**

He was born as the result of the **fervent** prayer of his parents to the **CREATOR.** He still remembers his mother spending hours in prayer along with the child in her lap. He has seen tears shedding from her eyes and when he asked her, she replied that she was **overwhelmed** by the love of the **HEAVENLY FATHER.** This left a deep desire in Mr. Sharma to **search for this HEAVENLY FATHER.** He studied all religious books in search of **HIM.**

During the second year of his graduate studies, from his college book, with hesitation he was reading the following day portion, <u>"**Sermon on the mount** ", which was part of the curriculum. It was mentioned that this Sermon on the Mount by **the LORD,** had a great impact on **Mahatma Gandhiji's life**</u>. It laid the foundation for his path of **nonviolence,** for Indian Freedom Movement. Then he recollected his days in **Gandhi's Ashram, and realised that Gandhiji's life was based on this Sermon. Gandhiji's Freedom**

Struggle was the essence of this Sermon. He mentioned that **Gandhiji** had the practice of reading this sermon every day and followed by Prayer. When Mr. Sharma read the **Be-Attitudes and Blessedness** part of the sermon, he felt someone talking to him. He saw a great light with brightness of **1000 suns** entering in his room. This is how **GOD** intervened in his life.

When Mr. Sharma spoke about his parents, he mentions that, they were righteous people, and their life was holy and was full of acts that pleased **GOD.** Likewise irrespective of caste, creed, religion and language, the eyes of the **"GOD OF RIGHTEOUS ,run to and fro, to intercept those who live in righteousness and their generation too, to take them to HIS GLORY."**

GIFT OF GOD

As for every man to whom GOD has given riches and wealth, and given him power to eat of it, to receive his heritage and rejoice in his labour –this is the gift of GOD. (Ecclesiastes: 5:19)

RIGHTEOUS LORD MOVING ON THE WHOLE EARTH, WHAT HE HAS DONE FOR THE RIGHTIOUS NATION?

1611, is the year **Great Britain** received a **Marvellous Light**. It is the year the first English translation of the-**"CREATOR'S LEGAL MANUAL"** entered into Britain. The people, who read this book with deep thirst, were stirred in their hearts, went around the world, building (i)Hospitals, (ii)Schools, (iii)Colleges, (iv)Orphanages, (v) Shelters for the poor, ----- and exhibited **God's** righteousness in their acts. **GOD saw the good works of the people**, so the amazing **righteousness of GOD descended** on their land. This small country got **empowered to rule** over the whole world. But today the same country has lost its **righteous-walk**, and placed **GOD'S Manual** in dark room and **HE** will bring everything into justice. (**Ecclesiastes – 12:14**)

(i). *For GOD will bring every work into judgement including every secret thing, whether good or evil.*
                    (Ecclesiastes – 12:14)
(ii).   Lord GOD loves the Righteous Nation that we can read in;
   "Righteousness   exalts   a   nation,   -----" .
(Proverbs 14:34)
(iii). *I was sought by those who did not ask for ME. I was found by those who did not seek ME. I said Here I am, here I am , To a nation that was   not called by My name.*
(Isaiah-65:1)
Daniel- 2:21 confirms the same.
(iv) *"And HE Changes the times and the seasons; He removes kings and raises up kings; He gives wisdom to the wise And knowledge to those who have understanding .*

FATHER OF LIGHT
IS SEEKING FOR THE LOYAL HEART

Every good gift and every perfect gift is from above ,and comes down from the Father of lights, with whom there is no variation of shadow of turning. (James-1:17)

Do not be deceived ,GOD is not mocked: for whatever a man sows, that he will also reap. (Galatians 6:7)

For every one who partakes only of milk is unskilled in the word of righteousness, for
he is a babe. (Hebrews 5:13)

"*GOD set the wicked one along slippery places and cast them down to destruction.* (Psalms: 73.3 to 19).

The treacherous world rose up against The Most Righteous One and step up, to throw Him down over the cliff. ----------"- Read (Luke 4:25 to 30.)

---

9. WHAT WILL HAPPEN WHEN ONE WALKS IN GOD'S RIGHTEOUSNESS

When the whole world was flooded in sexual sin, **GOD** decided to destroy the world through flood. But one **Noah,** found grace in the sight of **GOD**; and **GOD** said to **Noah,**

"----------- *I have seen that "you are righteous before ME in this generation."* (Genesis -7:1)

"And did not spare the ancient world, but saved Noah, one of eight people, a preacher of right- eousness, bringing in the flood on the world of the ungodly;" (2Peter 2:5)

Sodom and Gomorrah cities also went through the same destruction, because of their homosexual sin, and is recorded as

"And turning the cities of Sod'om and Gomor'rah into ashes, condemned them to destruction, mak- ing them an example to those who afterward would live ungodly." (2Peter 2:6)

When **the LORD** was crucified among the criminals, **one criticizes** but at the same time the other criminal speaks out as,

"And we indeed justly, for we receive the due reward of Our deeds; but this Man has done nothing wrong.
"   (Luke -23:41)

When the word of righteousness emerged out of his mouth, the **LORD** replied at once saying that **today you will be with me in Paradise.**"

WHO WILL UPHOLD THE UPRIGHT

"The steps of a good man are ordered by the Lord, And He delights in his way. "   (Psalm - 37:23)

Though he fall, he shall not be utterly cast down; For the Lord upholds him with His hand.   (Psalm - 37:24)

I have been young, and now am old; Yet I have not seen the righteous forsaken, Nor his descendants begging bread."   (Psalm - 37:25)

The great King David, throughout the full length of his life, observes his country-men, both righteous and wicked, but he sees that the wicked and his descendants are on the streets for food. At the same time the righteous one, and his descendants are not looking to anyone for their daily bread.

TO WHOM HIS EYES ARE ON
AND HIS EARS ARE OPEN?

(i) *"The eyes of the Lord are on the righteous, And His ears are open to their cry."*   (Psalm-34:15)

(ii)*" For the perverse person is an abomination to the LORD, But HIS secret counsel is with the upright".*
(Proverbs 3:32)

(iii). *The CURSE of the LORD is on the house of the wicked, But HE bless the home of the just.* (Pro.3:33)
HIGHEST MYSTERY OF "THE <u>CREATOR'S LEGAL MANUAL</u>!"

"And many lepers were in Israel in the time of E-li'sha the prophet, and none of them was cleansed except Na'a-man, the Syrian."
(Luke- 4:27)

Why **LORD** said like this in the New Testament; because the entire mystery of **the Creator's Legal Manual** is here. Please meditate **2Kings -5:1,** and one can understand that Army Chief Na'a- Man is, a **sincere, truthful, duty-conscious, upright, righteous** person. So **CREATOR LORD GOD, followed him and healed him**, given the outstanding exception from the **first Law.**

This we can see in **2Kings 5:18, 19**
Further 1 Timothy -1:9, and Luke- 4:27
to 30, Conforms the same

WHO WILL REST ON PEACE AND WHO HAS NO DEATH?

"Mark the blameless man, and observe the upright;For the future of that man is peace.
(Psalm- 37:37)
"In the way of righteousness is life, And in its pathway there is no death.
(Proverbs 12:28)

61

10. THE RIGHTEOUS WORKS THAT PLEASE GOD

The Creator's Legal Manual clearly distinguishes the righteous works of **HIS** creation that pleases **HIM,** that we see now.

1. WHO WILL BE EXALTED WITH HONOUR

"He has dispersed abroad, He has given to the poor: His righteousness endures forever; His horn will be exalted with honour." (Psalm- 112:9)

2. WHEN HE SHALL BE YOUR REAR GUARD

"Is it not to share your bread with the hungry, and that you bring to your house the poor who are cast out; When you see the naked, that you cover him, And not hide yourself from your own flesh?

(Isaiah- 58:7)

Then your light shall break forth like the morning, Your healing shall spring forth speedily, And your righteousness shall go before you; The glory of the Lord shall be your rear guard."

(Isaiah- 58:8)

Then you shall call, and the LORD will answer;You shall cry : and HE will say HERE I AM-- (Isaiah- 58:9)

If you extend your soul to the hungry And satisfy the afflicted soul , then your light shall Dawn in the darkness And your darkness shall be as the noonday . (Isaiah- 58:10)

3. WHICH IS MORE ACCEPTABLE TO GOD

HE stores up sound wisdom for the upright: HE is a shield to those who walk Uprightly.

(Proverbs-2:7)

The righteous man walks in his integrity: His children are blessed after him. (Proverbs-20:7)

To do righteousness and justice Is more acceptable to the Lord than sacrifice.

(Proverbs-21:3)

"For they being ignorant of GOD'S righteousness, and seeking to establish their own righteousness, have not submitted to the righteousness of GOD. (Romans-10:3)

Also Read Matthew 25:34to46, Luke10:30 to 35, Luke 14:13, 14 Luke16:19to23, Romans-2:11-16, Romans-10:20, Isaiah-65:1

Please listen to the words the **LORD -GOD** pours out to Humanity. Feed the hungry, for those who do not have proper dress **clothe** them, when you are positioned high help your blood relations. This kind of fasting pleases **HIM**. Not only that, seeing the righteous action, the **LORD GOD** says, your healing shall spring forth speedily. Your righteousness shall go before you and it will uphold you and **you will arise up.** In order to protect you, "The **invisible Arm of GOD will follow behind you".** So much, **LORD GOD** positioned **"Mercy and Righteousness** "and **HE Glorifies the same.**

63

11. LORD'S WARNING TO HUMAN RACE

All fruitless trees will be cut-off, split and then used for fire wood. On the contrary, fruit yielding trees will draw the direct attention and honour of the **Master.**

"A good tree cannot bear bad fruit, nor can a bad tree bear good fruit. (Matthew-7:18)

Every tree that does not bear good fruit is cut down and thrown into the fire. (Matthew-7:19)

Therefore by their fruits you will know them. "

(Matthew-7:20)

WILD TREE

This I will explain in detail. Let us look at a **wild tree that grows in the wilderness.** Because it is stronger and taller and stands at higher altitude, it roots out deeper both vertically and horizontally. It spreads out its branches and it sucks out the nutrients of the near ones and from neighbouring ones.

In the last days the country trees will become wild trees. The country tree positions itself in such a way it finds a root at high levels. Once strength and might are gained by the country tree, it will **emerge out as a wild tree**, grows to touch the sky and spreads out its branches worldwide. At the same time it sucks out the **nutrients** of fruit yielding trees. As it grows so high, it shades and thus prevents the light, directly falling on the fruit yielding trees and shortens its Life.

Moreover in order to suck the sap of the fruit yielding trees, it keeps them under its shadows. The fruitless wild tree which has so much might and power grows so high, with bulged girth- the **LORD GOD declares** how **HE** is going to deal with it, and it is recorded in **Matthew-**

7:-21-23.

Read it, understand it, and Conceive it. Look at the Depth And Decree Lord God Pronounced.

<u>FRUIT YIELDING TREE</u>

At the same time we will see a fruit yielding tree, say a coconut tree. When it starts yielding, its owner fences around the tree to protect it from **intruders.** Then he manures it with fertilizers through trenches around the tree, and also cleans its head from insects, dry, dead leaves etc. Why does the owner **prune** the tree? He prunes the tree to make it give more fruits. It is to make the tree to yield more, to be more fruitful to others.

In the same way GOD also prunes us, when we start yielding good fruit, in order to take us with Him, and keep with Him.

<u>DISREGARD TO THE MAJESTY OF THE LORD</u>

(i) *"Let grace be shown to the wicked, Yet he will not learn righteousness; In the land of uprightness he will deal unjustly, And will not behold the majesty of the Lord.* (Isaiah- 26:10)

(ii) *"Some men's sins are clearly evident, preceding them to judgement, but those of some men follow later* (1Timothy- 5:24)

Let me explain this. My friend who is on a journey met me and handed over to me **Rs. 5 lakhs,** to keep it safe until his return. After his return he approaches me for the money and if I refuse to pay, then my action is an **offence** for which the punishment is reserved. At the same time, my own sister who is poor has handed over her belongings, during her move to another place for a better Job. When she returns after few years, **she requested and then she begged** ----me for her belongings. If I deny at this juncture and act as though I have not received anything from her, it becomes a **severe offence**. To this only, **GOD** said such sins cannot wait for judgement until that day. **GOD** will settle in a beautiful righteous manner, according to the magnitude and severity of the pain induced to the blood relation. The **GOD'S** Judgment will knock the door the next day or within a short time.

(iii). *"Woe to her who is rebellious and polluted, To the oppressing city! "* (Zephaniah-3:1)

GOD is not referring to the filthiness in the streets of the city, but the filth in the lives of the people residing in the city.

All around the world we see people who live according to their own intentions and ways, without any fear of **GOD**. Thus they are ruining their own lives, and also the lives of others and the Country too.

(iv). ***"And there is no creature hidden from His sight, but all things are naked and open to the eyes of Him to whom we must give account."*** (Hebrews-4:13)

(v).----- The LORD, The LORD GOD,merciful and gracious ,longsuffering and abounding in goodness and truth,

Keeping mercy for thousands, forgiving iniquity and transgression and sin , by no means clearing the guilty,visiting the iniquity of the fathers upon the children and the children's children to the third and fourth generation. (Exodus-34-6,7)

Please be <u>understand</u> the depth of **HIS** vision and frighten to **HIS RIGHTEOUSNESS.**

WARNING TO YOUTH

"Rejoice, O young man, in your youth, And let your heart cheer you in the days of your youth; Walk in the ways of your heart, And in the sight of your eyes; But know that for all these God will bring you into judgment".

(Ecclesiastes - 11:9)

The wisest King born on earth with the wisdom, pronounced by **Lord-GOD** Himself, was *King Solomon.* **GOD** said that

"-------- I have given you a wise and understanding heart ,so that there has not been anyone like you before you nor shall any like you arise after you.

(1 kings 3:12)

He wrote these advance warning words to the younger generation, "O young man, You walk according to your will, walk in the sight of your eyes, But you should know one thing that, **the Lord God** will bring everything under justice".

I will explain this.

(i)   **GOD read your ancestors,**

(ii)   **Closely watching on your ways and your walk during the tenure of teenage.**

(iii)   **and He scans your mind thoughts and finally He fits,**

Houses and riches are an inheritance from fathers: But a prudent wife is from the Lord."
(Proverbs-19:14)

SKY AND EARTH ARE DATA BANK
OF EVERY   HUMAN

"For GOD will bring every work into judge-ment, Including every secret thing, Whether good or evil."   (Ecclesiastes – 12:14)

GOD is watching over each and every human being and his or her deeds, whether done in public or in secrecy. Each and every one of us would understand this truth. If we can go back and analyse our own lives, we all can acknow-ledge the <u>Righteous</u> **GOD's** <u>intervention</u>, in our lives and how **HE** manoeuvred too.

Though the husband and wife relationship is the most intimate relationship in its depth and intensity, where body and mind unite, in that relationship also the husband does not know what is going on in the wife's mind and the wife does not know what is going on in her hus-band's mind. But The ***GOD OF THE UNIVERSE*** knows the **thoughts of** all the people on the earth and **their dreams.**

HOW HE MONITORS OUR MIND
& TO   UNDERSTAND HIS DEPTH:

"He seals the hand of every man, -----"   (Read Job- 37:7)

SKY

GOD has given **bar Code** in the hands of everyone. A dish antenna of 2'- diameter installed over the terrace of our home is able to draw all the data from all over the world. But the **LORD- GOD** stretched out the **sky as dish antenna** and set it in position and through **bar code**, ie., the bar code on hand, the inner and outer of every one is scanned, and all secret things of every one are thus open to

GOD.

How is it possible? Yes. If we put together all the computers of the world, it can't be equal to even **a** chip of **GOD's** Computer and **HE** is **infinitely Omniscient.**

EARTH

Not only that at the same time, **earth** registers the foot- steps of every one, and also one's whereabouts in detail as said in,

---

(i). *"He shall call to the heavens from above, And to the earth, that He may judge His people."* (Psalm- 50:4)

(ii).*The heavens will reveal his iniquity, And the earth rise up against him.* (Jow:20:27)

(iii), *I call heaven and earth as witness today against you, that I have set before you life and death, blessing and cursing, therefore choose life, that both you and your descendants may live.* (Deuteronomy-(30-19)

So the Heaven and Earth are positioned *at* their own orbit as a witness, to report about the life of every one "at the time of Judgement."

LORD-GOD'S - GLORIOUS WARNING

Learn to do good: Seek justice. Rebuke the oppressor: Defend the fatherless, Plead for the widow. (Isaiah-1:17)

Who justify the wicked for a bribe, And take away justice from the righteous man.
(Isaiah-5:23, Result-read. Isaiah- 5:24)

For the stone will cry out from the wall, And the beam from the timbers will answer it.
(Habakkuk:-2:11)

Behold, the day of the Lord comes. Cruel, with both wrath and fierce anger, To lay the land desolate: And He will destroy its sinners from it. (Isaiah-13:9)

God who had made the world and everything in it, since HE is the Lord of heaven and earth, does not dwell in temples made with hands. (Acts 17:24)

Do not think I came to bring peace on earth. I did not come to bring peace but a sword. (Mathhew- 10:34)

Blind guides ,who strain out a gnat and swallow a camel. (Mathew 23:24)

A bruised reed He will not break, And smoking flax He Will not quench ,Till HE sends forth JUSTICE TO VICTORY.
(Mathew:12:20)

For the wrath of GOD is revealed from heaven against all ungodliness and unrighteousness of men, who suppress the truth in unrighteousness. (Romans-1:18)

PLEASE CONTINUE TO READ

(i) John-9:39. Matthew- 5:18-20, 7:13-15,   Mathew-
23:13 to-24.   21:31,32,   Luke-7:29.

(ii) Matthew-24:24. IITimothy-4:3,4. IIPeter-2:1 To 3.
IICorin.-11:13-15. Micah-2:11, 3:11. Ezekiel-34:17 to 22.

(iii) Matthew- 19:24. Mark -10:25. Luke-10:4, 12:33,34.
16:13, 18:25, Matthew-10:9 to 10. Mark-6:8 to 9.

(iv) Jeremiah- 7:4, 8:7-8, 4:22, 5:30-31, 6:10, 13.

(v) Isaiah-1: 10, 13, 15,17, 21, 23, 56:10,11,   Habakkuk :2-11, Ezekiel-13:17,18. Amos-6:3 to 5. Hosea-9:8,

(vi) Matthew-15:4 to 9. Isaiah 29:13, Proverbs- 21:3,
Hosea-6:6. Amos-4:4, 5. Haggai-2:11 to 14,Romans-1:18

IRRESPECTIVE OF CASTE, CREED, RELIGION, LAN-
GUAGE, ONE JUDGEMENT FOR EVERY ONE

Romans-2:11-16, 10:20. Isaiah-65:1.
James- 3:1, 5:1, 9. Psalm-96:13,

Psalm-98:9. Psalm-50:4, Revelation-20:13

12. END TIME EVENTS

We are in the Last Days. Let me illustrate that with the things happening around the world, by comparing the same with Human Life. The typical life span of a person is say 90 Years. It could be split into 3- Phases,

(i) 1-30 Years 1st Phase, (ii) 30-60 Years is middle or second, (iii) 60-90 the third or Last Phase. Let's examine the changes that happen in the human body during the last phase of our **earthly life,** and at the same time **we look deeply at the changes that are happening around us in the world in these last days.**

HUMAN BODY	WORLD
READ ⟹	The world is comprised of several Countries, every country has several Families. The nervous system are the families, and the brain of the family is the People.
(I). The Changes that happen in the body, in the **Last phase** are the weakening of the nervous system and in turn, **the brain** loses its memory.	Similarly in the last days the people of the world are growing in knowledge, but at the same time their brain function drops down to remember the **CREATOR.** ---------

(ii). In the last days, the nervous system of the human body loses its vigour and so physical movement weakens, and the footsteps will slow down.

Similarly, the country's nervous system are families. World in its last stage has lost its vigour of love, and so weakened in its family structure and the marriage foot steps are slowing down. That is why we read about the uncleanliness, increase in divorce rate, murder in family etc. and the **GOD**-designed marriage system is losing its sanctity and stepping down on its walk.

(iii). In the last phase, in the body blood pressure increases.

Similarly in the country, people in their urge to earn money, want to gain wealth, in a very short span of time and thus they are pressurised. Life pressure is increased.

(i.v). In the last days there are new diseases, several surgeries are performed in the body, like open heart surgery, kidney- transplantation, etc.. etc. In these ways, the body loses the blood and it weakens the body, and it moves towards the end time.

Similarly world around, inside the Country, there are cheating, rapes, suicides, murders, civil wars of various kinds etc. etc--- resulting large bloodsheds, across the land. Day by day these crime- rates are increasing at rapid rate, and the world is moving fast in its track to finish its race.

BEGINNING OF A NEW AGE:

1. CHANGE IN CHARACTER,
2. KNOWLEDGE
3. TONE IN SONGS------

1. CHANGE IN CHARACTER

Now we look into the changes that happen in the human character at the **beginning of this age**

But know this, that, "in the last days perilous times will come: (2Timothy -3: 1)

For men will be lovers of themselves , lovers of money, boasters, proud, blasphemers ,disobedient to parents,, unthankful, unholy, (2Timothy -3: 2)

Unloving, unforgiving, slanderers, without self-control brutal, despisers of good. (2Timothy -3: 3)

Traitors, headstrong, haughty, lovers of pleasure rather than lovers of GOD, . (2Timothy -3:4)

Having a form of Godliness, but denying its power. ------------" (2Timothy -3:5)

For I know your manifold transgressions
And your mighty sins: Afflicting the just and taking bribes;
Diverting the poor from justice at the gate.

(Amos -5:12)

Therefore the prudent keep silent at that time, For it is an evil time. (Amos -5:13)

You will all agree with me that we are observing the same thing in the world around us, but **GOD** has written this down several thousand years back.

2.INCREASE IN KNOWLEDGE

> "--------- *many shall run to and fro, and know-ledge shall increase.*" (Daniel; 12:4)

The world has shrunk and travel around the world for knowledge, fame, wealth etc. become easy. The knowledge is progressing day by day and in its vision world is brighter and brighter and it attracts more and more and thus **blocks and derails the righteous journey** towards the **CREATOR above.**

3.TONE IN SONGS-----

> "*And the songs of the temple Shall be wailing in that day, -------*", (Amos- 8:3)

At present days and seasons we are able to see such alarming songs well penetrate in, and attract the inner man. But the softness of the song or music is pleasing and moving up towards the light and the converse is pleasing and descending towards the darkness.

CONTINUOUS ORDERLY DISPLAY OF WARNINGS TO THE HUMAN RACE

HEAR OF WARS, EARTHQUAKES, FAMINES, PESTI-LENCES------

"*But when you hear of wars and commotions, do not be terri-fied: for these things must come to pass first; but the end will not come immediately.* (Luke- 21:9)

"*Then He said to them, Nation will rise against nation, and kingdom against kingdom.*" (Luke- 21:10)

"*And there will be great earthquakes in various places, and famines and pestilences; and there will be fearful sights and great signs from heaven.*" (Luke -21:11)

"And there will be signs in the sun, in the moon, and in the stars; and on the earth distress of nations, with perplexity, the sea and the waves roaring;" (Luke- 21:25)

All these events were revealed about 2000 years ago and recorded in the **CREATOR'S LEGAL MANUAL** and are becoming everyday reality.

NOW WE ARE EXPERIENCING
THE SIGNS IN LAND, IN WATER, SKY ETC.

(i). Sign in Land: Earth quake and its intensity scale increases in magnitude year by year, land sliding, volcanic eruptions etc. are taking place stage by stage and step by step.

(ii). Sign in water: Sea water level increases, and in deep sea beds the water current changes in its direction.

(iii) Sign in sky: Planets are coming on one line, Fire stone strikes the earth.

All these events are increasing in magnitude, year by year, indicating that whatever written in the manual is **true**.

(iv). SIGN IN SUN AND MOON:

Now, I'm sharing few inventions and newspaper articles that confirm the fulfilment of the **words** recorded in the **Creator's Legal Manual. Dhinamalar** dated 26/10/2003 reported the observance of **3.8 lakh km. diameter** dark spot in the **sun.** Malaimurasu article dated, 6/12/2011 reported that the size of this dark spot has increased. It also reported that the **moon** appeared **red** for 51 seconds.

"The sun shall be turned into darkness, And the moon into blood, before the coming of the great and awesome day of the LORD",   (Joel- 2:31)

All these events and changes are continuously taking place on the planet.

(v). APPEARANCE OF A NEW "DIAMOND PLANET"

In Aug, 2011, scientists have observed a new planet called **Diamond planet**. This planet is full of diamonds. Scientists declared that, this Planet is at a distance of **4000-light years**. The speed of light is 3 lakh km per sec. The distance travelled by the light in one Year is approximately **Million Crore** Km, and this distance is called **one light year**

one light year = $(9.46 \times 10^{\wedge}5) \times (10^{\wedge}7)$, Km.

See the glory of the **CREATOR**. The **Astrophysics Scientists** are unable to give more detail, and they simply say diamond planet appears **on space** at a distance of 4000 Light years.

GOD'S, Manual has already recorded regarding this diamond planet. This we see in the last book, **Revelation-21:10 & 11.**

"--------Great city-------- descending out of heaven from GOD,   (Revelation = 21:10)

Having the glory of GOD. Her light was like a most precious stone, like a jasper stone, clear as crystal. (Revelation- 21:11)

(vi) *ARISING QUESTION OF THE NEW AGE*

In the present day, youngsters have started asking a question, "**If GOD has created all things, who created GOD?**" Though we can clarify this question in several ways, we can't convince those until they personally experience **GOD**. I like to say one thing to those with such a question:

In every one's life old age will come, then one has to move to last days, and then end moment will arrive, at that time one who has this question can feel,

(vii).   <u>HE IS THE ANSWER</u>

NOW UNDERSTAND HIM, CREATOR ALONE IS

1. BEGINNINGLESS.
2. ENDLESS.
3. FORMLESS.
4. BOUNDARYLESS
5. IMMEASURABLE.
6. IMMORTAL.
7. EVER GLOWING
8. EVERLASTING and
9. **INFINITELY INFINITE.**

HOW TO BE NEARER TO HIS SPACE?

If anyone in his life is running to keep his committed words and timings with truth, then **THE CREATOR** of the Universe, will interfere in his track. This interference will track him to walk in **HIS** mercy and righteousness. Finally he will be treading towards **HIS SPACE**.

---

13. GLORY OF GOD'S CREATION

I have told in the end of previous chapter that Lord God, Creator is *INFINITELY INFINITE.* That we see now.

"GOD - IS THE SOURCE OF ALL ENERGIES."

The **Universe** in which we live was created by **the Creator** by **HIS Infinite Wisdom.** This we can see in **Genesis 1:1**

His Infinite, Omnipotent, Glorious Might keeps all the revolving Galaxies and stars in position, and **HE** fixed an orbit for each one of them. **No man has been able to understand the details regarding this Universe and its depth .** We will see now the steps and efforts taken by **Astrophysics Scientists,** to know the details of the Universe. I am sharing with you now the various details collected by me, through the **web site.**

This Universe is crowded with Galaxies. Stars in bulk numbers positioned in an approximate spherical form are called **"Galaxy".**

In 1999 scientists declared that there are **12,500, crore,** Galaxies, present In the Universe.

Because of the developments in the field of **Astrophysics**, and the invention of **Radio Telescope fitted with x-ray cameras**, the Astrophysics Scientists have been able to see the space in depth. Previously the location appears to be indistinct, where Galaxies are visible. Now with the help of **German Super Computer**, Scientists have declared that there are about **50, 000, Crore** Galaxies in the

Universe. Scientists are unable to give the exact number. Galaxies are not uniform in size. Small Galaxy contains approximately **one million stars**, and big Galaxy contains **one trillion stars**. On an average there are **one billion stars** per Galaxy.

MILKY WAY GALAXY

The Galaxy we live is called the Milky Way Galaxy. This Galaxy contains approximately **40,000 Crore** stars. Out of this the sun, the moon, the earth are but a few of them. *At this Juncture please observe the Amazing GOD'S MIGHT in creation.*

The Milky Way Galaxy Contains three Parts.
1. The outer spherical distribution contains stars,
2. The central disk,
3. The disk's nucleus Centre is bulged out and it is the Galactic Centre.

The diameter of the Milky Way galaxy is approximately **One lakh light years.** We have already seen one light year is approximately **million-crore km.**

In order to conceive the distance, please consider one travels in air at a speed of **1500km/hour.** The period required to cross one light year is approximately **7 lakh years.** At the same time, the period required to cross the Milky Way is **7000 crore years.**

If so, what a man can understand about the Universe, with just a life span of 80 years. With all available technology, It is not possible to view **A Galaxy in full**, if so how to analyze **50,000 Crore Galaxies.**

Now we approximately estimate the no. of **Stars** at present available In the Universe.

On an average one Galaxy contains **one billion stars** multiplied by **50, 000 crore Galaxies**

$$= (100 \times 10^7) \times (50,000 \times 10^7)$$
$$= 5 \times (1000 core) \times (1000 crore) = (5) \times 10^{20}$$

This can't be counted by any number of people over any period of time.

But **GOD**:

"He counts the number of the stars; He calls them all by name." (Psalm-147:4)

"He alone spreads out the heavens, And treads on the waves of the sea." (Job - 9:8)

All the galaxies are revolving around HIM and HIS presence (HIS SPIRIT) is shadowing the Universe.

Such A Mighty Creator, How can we praise **HIM**.
HE is:

1. **OMNIPOTENT**
2. **OMNISCIENT**
3. **OMNIPRESENT**
4. **OMNIENERGIZER**

Now please see the videos of the Milky Way Galaxy, **(Video ref. page-3)** and see **The CREATOR, LORD, GOD'S Might** and **Glory**, and please conceive it in heart and mind.

ONE WHO Created the 50, 000 crore Galaxies and what one can understand about the **Galaxy Zone** which we have seen just now?

HE stretches out the north over empty space; HE hangs the earth on nothing. (Job.26:7)

"HE has made the earth by HIS power, HE has established the world by HIS wisdom, And has stretched out the heavens at HIS discretion. " (Jeremiah -10:12)

" HE turned the rock into a pool of water, The flint into a fountain of waters. (Psalm-114:8)
His Glorious creation reveals **HIS migh**t, which we see in

"The heavens declare the glory of GOD; And the firmament shows HIS handiwork." (Psalm-19.1)

So Great is HIS Might to carry 50, 000 crore Galaxies and its stars, each one of size as sun, moon, earth etc. and weighing multibillion tonnes each, have been positioned in its orbit. How much easy it is for **HIM** To fix an orbit for a human of about 80kg. But **HE** permits us to swing according to our free-will, on our own ways in an open orbit, even then **HE** is in search of us, and we stand alive before Him, because of **HIS Infinite Mercy.**

14. GLORY OF GOD'S RIGHTEOUSNESS

In any country if, righteousness and justice are in order among the people of the land and the people in power; then for such country the **sunlight** and the **rain** are up to the pleasing level in the respective seasons, to meet the requirement of the land. The actual scene is in,

He who builds His layers in sky, And has founded His strata in the earth; Who calls for the waters of the sea, And pours them out on the face of the earth.The LORD is HIS name.   (Amos-9:6)

I know your manifold transgressions and your mighty sins: afflicting the just and taking bribes: Diverting the poor from justice at the gate.   (Amos-5:12)

SO LORD, GOD SAYS:

" *I also withheld rain from you, When there were still three months to the harvest. I made it rain on one city; I withheld rain from another city. One part was rained upon, And where it did not rain the part withered.*   (Amos- 4:7)

So two or three cities wandered to another city to drink water, But they were not satisfied; Yet you have not returned to me." Says the LORD."   (Amos-4:8)

AUTOMIZATION FOR HIS PIVOTED JUDICIARY

Further, "HE Automized And Energized HIS Pivoted Judiciary, Below On And Above Earth". That we will see now in Job-28:26, 37:11 to 13.

"----HE made a law for the rain, And a path for the thunderbolt", (Job -28:26)

Also with moisture HE saturates the thick clouds; HE scatters HIS bright clouds: (Job - 37:11)

And they swirl about, being turned by HIS guidance, That they may do whatever HE commands them On the face of the whole earth. (Job -37:12)

HE causes it to come, Whether for correction, Or for HIS land, Or for mercy." (Job -37:13)

LORD makes the moisture to rise up as clouds and is, moving in space carrying **HIS Mercy and Righteousness.** Lightning scatters the dry clouds and the wet clouds and are swirling on the face of the whole earth according to the mercy and righteousness of the people of that terrain. **HE** determines which part of that country should **prosper** or **suffer** in **famine,** accordingly they stand still in space, and on **HIS** *commands* the cloud yields the **droplets.**

When very few people in a particular locality of a country live in mercy and righteousness, then they are fit to receive grace in the sight of **GOD.** Under such circumstances, the entire locality will prosper cloud drops, the ground water yields, and lakes and reservoirs just fill over. The air flow becomes breeze and the earth, trees and plants will yield and in turn the land will flourish.

At the same time, when the people of a particular locality are totally flooded in **grave sins**, then that locality will lose grace in the sight of **GOD**, and as a result, they reap heavy floods, landslides, breaching of the tanks, reservoirs and the water body turned in to ice. Alternatively there will be no rain, the sun will be hot and so the flow of air becomes hot tempest, so the earth trees and plants will be dried, resulting in famine and so on.

THUS LORD, GOD EXECUTES HIS RIGHTEOUS-NESS, BELOW ON AND ABOVE THE EARTH.

FURTHER LORD'S RIGHTEOUSNESS EXTENDS FROM WOMB TO GRAVE AND TO THAT DAY.

(a).IN WOMB:
"Your *eyes saw my substance, being yet unformed. And in Your book they all were written, The days fashioned for me, When as yet there were none of them."* (Psalm-139:16),

(i), In the womb, the communication between eye to brain, ear to brain, to form all the other organs etc, **and to fix gender,** are not by the might of the parents, but it is the merciful perusal of the past history of the family keeping **HIS MERCY and RIGHTEOUSNESS** in front and tracking **HIS EYES** on the path of the couple and thus the body parts are moulded and shaped in. **NOW UNDERSTAND HIS MIGHT IN CREATION.**

(ii), How HE would mould the offspring of the righteous one, please read **Job-42:15, and know it and conceive it.**

NOW TRY TO UNDERSTAND THE DEPTH OF HIS MANUAL AND THUS UNDERSTAND HIM.

(b). IN GRAVE:

In the book of 1 Kings Chapter 21, we see a **Queen Esabel.** She lived an erratic life and at the same time she went to apex in pride. She was very bold enough to kill a righteous one for a piece of land. She setup witness against him and **stoned him to death.** Thus she took the possession of the land and added the same with her Palace. But at last, when we see her end, it is a great lesson to **humanity. When people went to bury her, they found her skull, leg, and hands and nothing more,** and her body was a meal for dogs. This we can see in **2kings 9:35.**

ELISHA:

At the same time we see the Prophet **Elisha** in the book of 2nd Kings. One notable woman told her husband, that the **Prophet** who passes that way, is found to be a **Holy Man.** But the **Prophet** died in **sick- bed.** Why such an end for a righteous man or righteous people, and this question arises among the minds of mankind.

For this we can see the answer in the "CREATOR'S LEGAL MANUAL."

"------ *The righteous will be recompensed on the earth,*
------ (Proverbs -11:31)

But when we are judged, we are chastened by the Lord, that we may not be condemned with the world.
" (1Corinthians-11:32)

At the same time **a human of the human** died and his body was taken to the graveyard.

So it was, as they were burying a man, that suddenly they spied a band of raiders: and they put the man in the tomb of E-li'sha and when the man was let down and touched the bones of E-li'sha he revived and stood on his feet.

(2kings-13:21)

Thus the name of the prophet is glorified by **GOD**.

The details, I have spoken and recorded, clearly reveal the Righteousness of **GOD** at all stages of human **life**. Likewise **LORD - GOD** performs **HIS** Righteousness from womb to grave, **Further to That Day.**

(Malachi- 3:5, Psalm-50:4, Revelation-20:13, Daniel-12:3, Matthew- 13:43)

15. ESSENCE OF THE CREATOR'S LEGAL MANUAL

Further His Righteousness continues up to that day, ie., the day of Judgement. As I mentioned earlier, **the essence** of a book will be present in the concluding chapter that we see now.

" *He who is unjust, let him be unjust still ; he who is filthy,let him be filthy still ; he who is righteous, let him be righteous still; he who is holy, let him be holy still.* (Revelation -22:11)

And behold, I am coming quickly, and My reward is with Me, to give to everyone according to his work." (Revelation -22:12)

The unjust is opposite of righteous and filthy is opposite of holiness. The essence of **this book** can be summarized into two, ie. **Righteousness** and **Holiness** . **HE** is nearing to one who walks in **HIS** mercy and righteousness, and when **HE** embraces, holiness is added and such one will be nearing to **HIS SPACE.**

When any one on this earth realizes that there is a **GOD,** that **HE exists** and **HE is infinitely righteous,** then at this stage the **Glorious Light (GOD of GLORY)** graciously follows him. Due to that, whenever he runs towards sinful ways, he senses the **HAND of GOD,** intercepting and chastising in hIs ways. So he leaves sinful ways and turns about to run on **GOD's** righteous track. One who does not sense **HIS Hand** runs continuously on his own self righteous track.

For they being ignorant of GOD'S right-eousness, and seeking to establish their own righteousness, have not submitted to the righteousness of GOD. (Romans-10:3)

No man can become holy by his own effort.
1. John 5:17, Says

"All unrighteousness is sin-------".
So righteousness will lead to holiness.

Now we see Hebrews, 5:13,

"For every one who partakes only of milk is un-skilled in the word of righteousness, for he is a babe."

When any one on this earth starts to walk in his baby steps in righteousness, the **Holy GOD** will lift him up and embrace him with **HIS Right Hand (Without the know-ledge of the individual)** and **HE** carries him to walk on further and further in his mercy and righteousness, and finally **GOD HIMSELF** re**veals**, then one would march from holiness to holiness,

"TO MEET
THE LORD
IN HIS GLORY."

16. LORD PRE-ORDAINED THIS MESSAGE TO TELL HIS GLORY TO THE HUMAN RACE

I am not a Preacher, but I am a Civil engineer by profession. When I look back at my own life, I felt that the **Lord** is a **Great, Righteous CREATOR. Then God's intervention** started in my life and **HE** made me to understand the greatness of **"His Might and Omnipotence"**. Not only that, **HE** called me by name, **"Now I am seeing <u>who is Mr. Paul Das. Mr. Paul Das in the name of the LORD</u>   I am seeing you. -------- started like this and end with -------, The LORD's Word is the staff that makes you to stand. You get up and walk"**. This word of prophecy said by **GOD'S** Prophet,   **N. Sathu Paul Solomon**, on 29-8-2009.

This Message is a fulfilment of the above said "Prophecy." View

Video: facebook : "godcreatorbook"
YouTube: " GOD CREATOR BIRTH OF THE BOOK"

Lord led me to give one message. It is incorrect to say **HE** led to a message and actually **HE** pulled me through to give this message. For that **GOD again** sent **HIS** loving one **John Dhas**. He came to my office building for his work. He met me during Feb.2012 in my office regarding his official work. When I started to explain "the **LORD'S WORD"**, immediately he called me to give a message.

I refused; **GOD** chastised me and pulled me through. How did that happen? I am a diabetic patient; I was taking a **scheduled drug** for the last 15 years. But till Feb. 2012, when I was using that medicine for my **sugar p**roblem, I was active. But on the same week, when I refused to give the message, that medicine became ineffective. I was moving closer to death. The **LORD** led me through my wife towards a **very righteous Doctor,** thro' whom I was miraculously cured. Then I called the "**Man of GOD** that I am going to give the message. **As LORD -GOD planned already, the thoughts have come to my mind and are became this Message.**

"---------I will not leave you until I have done what I have spoken to you."   (Genesis-28:15}

"I am nothing, but

ALL GLORY AND HONOUR BE TO

THE INFINITELY INFINITE, MERCIFUL,

"LORD - GOD",

**WHO ALONE HAS IMMORTALITY
DWELLING IN UNAPPROACHABLE LIGHT**

HAVING INFINITELY INFINITE

**MERCY AND RIGHTEOUSNESS
IN HIS HAND.**

17. SACRIFICE OF
"CREATOR AS SAVIOUR"

Lastly human race failed to understand the **Love of the HEAVENLY FATHER** , when they start to walk in their own **wicked** ways.

To show His **everlasting** love and to prove His **deep love**, the **CREATOR** came down from heaven to earth. Like a hen that gathers her chicks under her wings, **HE** called the humanity. **(Matthew-23:37)**

But people, because of false pride over wealth, **dare to do evil** and **disorderly thirst in life**, are led to dizziness, and in that condition they are unable to understand **HIM** as **FATHER**, and unrighteously **nailed HIM, nailing HIM, and going on nailing HIM. (Hebrews-6:6)**

The eagle is encircling at a very high altitude sharply watching a chicken, roaming on its own, not listening to the mother's call.

In an unexpected hour, the eagle attacks at a dashing speed and catch it and flies up. **The dizzy chick without knowing its position and what is ahead, enjoys and enjoys in the air.**
Likewise the Prince of this world is happily watching the human lives, getting destroyed in their own ways. The human race is unmindful of being out of shelter, fails to see the **CREATOR** above, but keeps looking at the ground, adding earth on earth, gold on gold, and not only that they run behind those **Worldly**

Great People, who come around city after city and find shelter under them. **Worldly Great people** are one who fail to live at the level of the lowest one **who has contributed to his growth.**

But **HE spreads out HIS HANDS** and calls the humans **to come Under HIS ARMS** for shelter.

IF HE COULD HAVE LIFTED HIS HANDS
HUMANITY WOULD HAVE GOT DESTROYED

<u>Now we see what happened when</u>
HE spreads out HIS HANDS.

"Then, *behold, the veil of the temple was torn in two from top to bottom; and the earth quaked and the rocks were split*

(Matthew -27:51)

And the graves were opened; and many bodies of the saints who had fallen asleep were **raised."** (Matthew -27: 52)

In order to find the shelter under the shadow of the **"CREATOR OF THE UNIVERSE",**

please open **HIS Manual** and then one can see the way to enter, and one can understand, be safe and be a Partaker of *HIS GLORY.*

"He who follows
righteousness and mercy
Finds life, righteousness and honour."

(Proverbs- 21:21)

This booklet is a message preordained by the LORD. As it speaks of HIS mercy and HIS righteousness, HIS invisible and merciful Arm pulls the righteous one towards HIM, irrespective of caste, creed, religion, language---- To deliver the righteous, HIS GLORY, is raining as a mist, and is moistening the earth sphere. They will not sense either the intensity of the coming pestilence nor the swirl flood, whirlwind, heat of the burning fire or coming solar heat rays, but find " life, righteousness and honour" in HIM.

Also read: Micah 6:8, Hosea 12:6
Matthew 23:23)
Luke-7:29, Mathew-21:31, 32, Prov: 12:28,
Roma-10:3, 10:20, Isaiah- 65:1, Matthew-10:34,
John-9:39,   Hebrews-6:1to8,   Psalm-101:6,
Psalm-50:4, Psalm-41:1 to 3, Prov: 22-22, 23, Matthew-25:46, Daniel: 12:3, Matthew-13:43, Revela-20:13,

"ALL GLORY and HONOUR be to
HIM and **HIM** only."
AT LAST

HE WHO OVERCOMES **SHALL INHERIT** ALL THINGS, AND I WILL BE HIS **GOD** AND HE SHALL BE **MY- SON** (REVELATION-21:7)

GOD'S personal intervention, I have written all the pages of this book. The proof for **HIS** intervention is the video in YouTube, and Facebook. But today 21-11-2014, Friday evening at 6.00 P.M. while **uploading** the video to facebook, I have understood that not only **HE** is the source of all **ENERGIES,** but also the flow of every **electron, neutron, proton** etc, etc, also take directions along the dimensions ordered by **HIM** and **HIM** only. **(Read Job 28:26, Chapter 14).** So those who understand **HIS HEART AND MIGHT** while reading this book can certainly experience **HIS miraculous touch, in the areas for which one is longing.**

FACE BOOK: "godcreatorbook"
YouTube: "GOD CREATOR BIRTH OF THE BOOK"
                  (VIDEO ONLY)

JUDICIARRY ACTIVITY
ON THE EARTH
SURFACE
&
THE JUDICIARY IN SPACE
READ
THE FLOW CHART
IN THE NEXT
PAGE

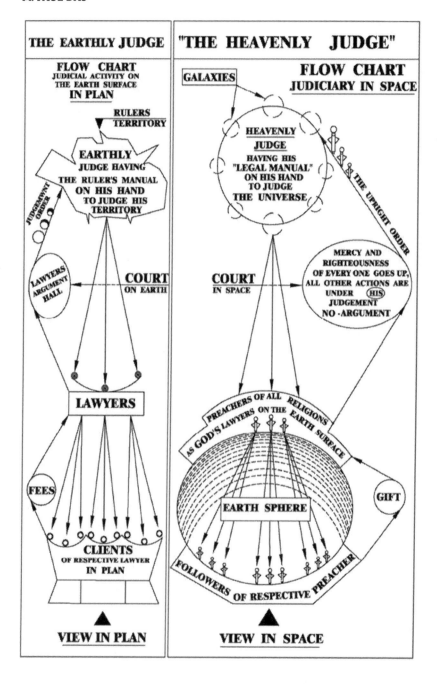

THE EARTHLY JUDGE

"THE HEAVENLY JUDGE"

FLOW CHART
JUDICIAL ACTIVITY ON
THE EARTH SURFACE
IN PLAN

GALAXIES

FLOW CHART
JUDICIARY IN SPACE

RULERS
TERRITORY

HEAVENLY
JUDGE
HAVING HIS
"LEGAL MANUAL"
ON HIS HAND
TO JUDGE
THE UNIVERSE

EARTHLY
JUDGE HAVING
THE RULER'S MANUAL
ON HIS HAND
TO JUDGE HIS
TERRITORY

JUDGEMENT ORDER

THE UPRIGHT ORDER

LAWYERS
ARGUMENT
HALL

COURT
ON EARTH

COURT
IN SPACE

MERCY AND
RIGHTEOUSNESS
OF EVERY ONE GOES UP,
ALL OTHER ACTIONS ARE
UNDER (HIS)
JUDGEMENT
NO-ARGUMENT

LAWYERS

PREACHERS OF ALL RELIGIONS
AS GOD'S LAWYERS ON THE EARTH SURFACE

FEES

GIFT

CLIENTS
OF RESPECTIVE LAWYER
IN PLAN

EARTH SPHERE

FOLLOWERS OF RESPECTIVE PREACHER

VIEW IN PLAN

VIEW IN SPACE

GOD'S MIGHT
AND GLORY
ON HIS CREATION

DIAMOND PLANET

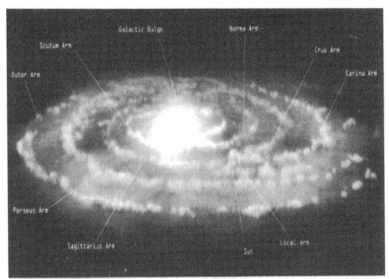

MILKY WAY VIEW

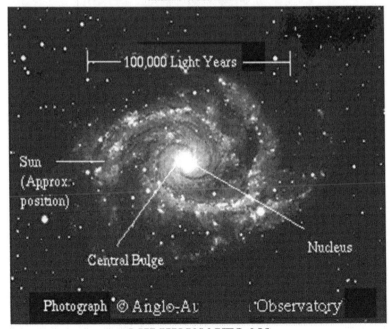

MILKY WAYPLAN

"GOD- CREATOR AS SAVIOUR"
IS MY DAD!

The penniless pauper is carried on your
Shoulder with utmost affection!

Though you smell the foul odour with in me
And from me, even then You kiss me!

Embrace with Your loving Hands
even when I am vomiting!

One who realizes that mercy and
righteousness are Your Ways, then Your
Legal Manual as a honeycomb
squeezed and fed to thee. !

Only one message of Your Heart to stir the
whole sphere is prophesied and given as

GOD- CREATOR OF THE UNIVERSE
HIS LEGAL MANUAL!

Thy Presence is in front to
accomplish the same

One Who rules the Universe

"CREATOR AS SAVIOUR" is my Dad!
DADDY! DADDY!! DADDY!!!

BE ENLIGHTENED TO MEET THE CREATOR

Now the hand of the man is tracking, the route of running vehicles and also of the living beings, if microchip is embedded in.

Man by his ability to sense the quake, how much more **"THE CREATOR HAND"**, can track and sense the quake of *all celestial, fleshly, botanic bodies and all living beings.*

GOD-CREATOR is infinitely perfect in *"HIS Mercy and righteous TRACK "*, to fix timings for the functioning and running of **ALL THE ABOVE**, on the earth and below and the length and destiny of **all** and **ALL.**

AS HE WATCHES (Psalm-121:3), be watchful and vigilant to run on the righteous track, individually defined by HIM, to receive the result of **Mercy** and **Righteousness** from **HIS HAND.**

M. Paul Das. *(1 Corinthians 1:27)*
Author and Structural Engineer.

Made in the USA
Columbia, SC
07 March 2023

13266181R00057